Bullseye:
Perceptive Reflections on a Collapsing Culture

By

William F. Harrell

Bullseye:
Perceptive Reflections on a Collapsing Culture

Copyright © 2013 by William Harrell

ISBN 978-1-939283-08-5

All rights reserved. No part of this book may be reproduced or transmitted in any form or by any means, electronic or mechanical, including photocopying, recording or by any information storage and retrieval system, without the written permission of the authors or publisher, except for the inclusion of brief quotations in a review or article, when credit to the book, publisher, and order information are included in the review or article.

Unless otherwise indicated, all Scripture taken from the King James Version of the Holy Bible.

Printed in the United States of America by Lightning Source, Inc.
Cover Design: Jessica Anglea www.jessicaanglea.com
Text design by Debbie Patrick, Vision Run, www.visionrun.com

Free Church Press
P.O. Box 1075
Carrollton, GA 30112

Contents

Foreword 5

Dedication 6

Section One: Our Collapsing Culture 7

Chapter 1: A Recipe for Ruin 9

Chapter 2: A Rose by Any Other Name 15

Chapter 3: Absolutes and Diversity 17

Chapter 4: Another Attack on Christianity 19

Chapter 5: Cloning is Here! 23

Chapter 6: Confused, Convoluted Christianity 27

Chapter 7: In Trouble 33

Chapter 8: Islam and Government 39

Chapter 9: Living in the Overload Zone 43

Chapter 10: Mirroring the Gravity of the Cross 47

Chapter 11: Perseverance or Preservation? 51

Chapter 12: The Abuse of Heaven 55

Chapter 13: The Firewall 57

Chapter 14: The Implications of Obedience 61

Chapter 15: The North Star of Society 63

Chapter 16: The Peace Prophecy Brings 67

Chapter 17: The Sinister Nature of Small Sins 69

Chapter 18: The Straw that Broke the Camel's Back 73

Chapter 19: The Translation Craze 77

Chapter 20: Think About This 81

Chapter 21: This Thing Called Transparency 85

Chapter 22: Two Different Stories with
Two Different Reactions 89

Chapter 23: Virtues are Still Virtues 93

Chapter 24: We Are Right and You Must Agree 97

Chapter 25: What It Was, Was a Toothpick 103

Section Two:
Quick Quotes and Pithy Sayings by William F. Harrell 107

Quick Quotes and Pithy Sayings 109

Section Three:
Inspirational Poetry by Elizabeth Greer Harrell 135

"Deep Down in the Heart" 137

"Here's Your Daughter, Mr. Thrift" 140

"Make Me A Promise Granddaddy" 143

"The Key" 144

"Your Last Day" 146

Other Books by Free Church Press 149

Foreword

Those of us who have known and loved Bill Harrell through the years have affectionately referred to him both privately and publicly as "The General." He is always leading and out in front of the rest of us ... and, like King David, he leads with "the integrity of his heart and the skillfulness of his hands."

This volume you hold in your hands is appropriately entitled *Bullseye: Perceptive Reflections on a Collapsing Culture* because it comes from one who has spent a lifetime hitting the bullseye. Bill pulls no punches here and deals head on with so many issues of life and faith that are easily avoided by too many others.

His reputation is spotless and his character is beyond reproach. He is and has always been in the middle of the target theologically. He writes these words not as pretty platitudes; he has beaten out these principles on the anvil of personal experience across the years.

Tolerance in our culture used to mean that we recognized and respected other's faith claims without accepting them. This volume puts the cultural collapse of the western world in the middle of the bullseye. We live in a world which now defines tolerance in such a way that all faith claims should be accepted as equal.

But don't take my word for it ... jump in now ... read it and reap!

O. S. Hawkins
President/CEO
GuideStone Financial Resources

Dedication

Every man who is called by God to be a Preacher of the Word and a Pastor to His People must have a faithful helpmate to stand alongside him during those years of service. This little tome is dedicated to my wife Carolyn because she has been that Godly helpmate for me. She has been a stabilizing force in the ministry that the Lord gave to me. Her help at crucial times has been invaluable to me. She has contributed much more to my ministry than any church member could ever know. I thank the Lord for bringing her into my life and for His blessings that continue to flow to me and to God's People through her.

Section One:
Our Collapsing Culture

Chapter 1

A Recipe for Ruin

For those people with a discerning eye, it is not difficult to discern that much of the world would like for the United States to simply vanish. In fact, they would take delight in being a part of the destruction of our society and way of life. The people who are most bent on destroying us are people who do not like a society in which the people are free. While freedom is a Biblical principle and valued by the hearts of men everywhere, the people who hate us want a country where people are ruled over and oppressed. It is difficult to imagine why anyone would prefer a society where only one or at most a few rule the lives of the people. The wealth of such a nation resides in just a few individuals while the rest of the populace cowers in poverty and oppression. They don't want the people to be free. They don't desire that they be free thinkers who can form their own opinions and set their own course for life. People like that cannot be ruled over and dominated.

So, many of the nations of the world hate the U.S. because we are the model for freedom. Their object is to destroy our country and way of life. One of the leading Muslim leaders said that the conquest of the United States was their goal. He stated that our form of government which is by the people and for the people, would be replaced by a caliphate. Make no mistake about it ...

there are those who have our destruction as a goal and the years involved are of no consequence to them.

If that is the goal, how would it be accomplished? It could never be done by war. We are the dominant military force on the globe. How could it happen? What would be the process by which one could make America fall piece by piece so that she would never know that it had happened until it was too late? The destruction of America would have to take place from within just as it occurred with Rome. I hate to say it but we are beginning to look like the Thanksgiving Turkey who has been cooked according to the Recipe for Ruin. Just a little more and you can "stick a fork" in the United States because it will be done.

How would one destroy America? Several things come to mind which, if not corrected, would result in the destruction of America from within.

First, remove God from the public arena. Our founding fathers who penned our constitution never meant for Christ and Christianity to become a main target for liberal moral degenerates to treat so disrespectfully. The liberals would have you believe that our founders were not Christian and that they had no concept of the fact that they were founding a Christian nation. From our very earliest documents we discover that the Pilgrims and early settlers stated that they were founding a nation to propagate the Gospel of Jesus Christ. If one is intellectually honest with themselves, and if they read our founding documents, then they will have to admit that Christians founded America with the idea that it would be a Christian nation. If I were the one seeking to destroy America from within I would remove God from the public arena and I would silence the pulpits; bring then under control by fear and intimidation and threaten them with monetary and legal consequences. I would tell the preachers that they should not be involved in politics even though Joseph preached to Potiphar, Moses preached to Pharaoh, Elijah preached to Ahab, Daniel preached to Belshazzar, Nathan preached to David, John preached to Herod

Antipas and Peter and John preached to the religious and political leaders of their day.

God intended for His people to have leaders who would show them the right way and lead them in it. Satan knows that he can succeed with much of his agenda of destroying America from within if he can get God's servants silenced.

Secondly, I would appoint liberal judges to write law from the bench. The Supreme Court desperately needs to be overhauled when it can't make up its mind on the Ten Commandments or abortion. Our constitution originated in the minds of men who recognized God for who He is. It is now being interpreted in a secular way by secular minded judges. That is the reason it is being warped the way it is. Just think of the number of cherished values which have been twisted out of shape by liberal judges. There was a completely wrong ruling on life when the court said that abortion is legal. The rulings on freedom of expression which have turned the pornographers and purveyors of immorality loose on society are a good example of how a liberal, secular mind can warp the Constitution's intentions.

So, if I were wanting to destroy America from within, I would surely appoint liberal judges to write law from the bench, allowing them to overturn the stated wishes of millions of voters in order to advance a liberal interpretation of the law.

Thirdly, I would adopt multiculturalism as our model. I would let people come to America and maintain their society in little pockets even to the point that their law could supersede our constitutional statements. I would also allow them to continue to use their own language while not demanding that English be the standard. Surely, I would not ask then to adopt our American ways. Taxes would be something that the vast majority of them would not have to be concerned with. In other words, if I wanted to destroy America I would downplay who we are and allow multiculturalism to become dominant thereby destroying the identity of the United States. The demand that people be Americans would diminish being replaced with tacit approval of multiculturalism.

Fourthly, I would fail to protect our borders. I would allow any and all illegal immigrants to come to the U.S. with impunity. Sending them home when caught would not be a priority thereby encouraging them to flood the country with thousands more. Then, of course, we should give them Social Security and other benefits that they did not earn but which they come to expect. Giving them the right to vote would also be on the agenda so that they could help shape the country in their image. Never mind that they don't want to prove their citizenship. Never mind that they don't own property. And, even though they can't prove their citizenship, I would give them a driver's license and other such privileges. Oh, yes, and I would not support American citizens when they try to do something about all of these things.

In the fifth place, I would give up our sovereignty over our country and our affairs. In fact, I would lead the country to take into consideration the legal precedents of Europe and Canada when interpreting our own constitution. It would also be necessary to make sure we did not hurt the feelings of the world community by insisting that our legal rulings be based on our own constitution. In order to do this it would be necessary to abandon our own constitution as our sole guide for all our legal standings and rulings. The movement to interpret our constitution in light of the legal rulings in other countries would be seen as a great advancement in our understanding of how we should relate legally to other countries. The idea that we are governed by our constitution alone would have to be jettisoned. This would allow for other legal systems such as Sharia law to be allowed to function within our borders as a recognized legal system. Basically this would diminish the position of our own constitution and make us like any other nation in the world. We would lose our unique place among nations. This would certainly play a part in the Recipe for Ruin.

If I wanted to bring America to ruin from the inside out, I would, in the sixth place, allow immorality to flourish under the guise of freedom. Our founders never meant to protect pornography. To say that they did is to dishonor them. If they could speak today they would defend themselves against those who say their writings make room for such immoral behavior. Our founders would have recoiled at the display of raw sex today under "freedom of expression." Those countries in the past which allowed immorality to flourish in every way ceased to exist. They died from within and they fell because of internal moral corruption. People have become so consumed with their freedoms that they have put themselves in bondage. Our first amendment rights were penned by Christians and they are being interpreted today by secularists and that will not work. It will only result in internal rottenness and failure. But, allowing immorality under the guise of freedom is an essential ingredient of the Recipe for Ruin.

Finally, in the seventh place, I would increase the national debt to unsustainable levels. This would mean that the country would have to borrow more and more money in order to keep up its standard of living. Ultimately, the crushing level of debt would result in an economic catastrophe which would sap away our financial strength and place us at the mercy of those from whom we had borrowed. A country which allows itself to become trapped in the vicious cycle of indebtedness will fall from within. So, if I wanted to destroy America from within, I would lead her into a tremendous level of debt which was unsustainable and when that debt reached and exceeded the annual GNP, the Recipe for Ruin would be virtually complete.

Does any of this look familiar? It should because these are some of the things our leaders have put in place over the past few years. America doesn't really need any enemies because her own leaders are concocting the perfect Recipe for Ruin. And our people are eagerly consuming it to their own peril and destruction.

Chapter 2

A Rose by Any Other Name

On many occasions, I have heard a preacher refer to God's "permissive will." Recently a pastor who was considering a serious ministerial move told me something like this, "I may not be in God's perfect will but I believe that I am in His "permissive will". In reply, I said, "So, you are going to settle for something less than God's perfect will?" His answer was "yes." As I studied over the implications of this situation, I began to try to discern just what this "permissive will" of God really is and I think that He has shown me something which everyone needs to recognize.

First, God's will is God's will, period. There are no degrees to His will because that would imply that He really didn't have his mind made up on something or that His will would fluctuate with facts and actions which He did not totally foresee. If God is omniscient, and He is, then there is nothing withheld from His knowledge. His will is not based upon what He sees that we are going to do, it is based upon what He knows will happen.

Secondly, "permissive will" says that a person can decide which level of God's will they will reside in as if to say that they are still within the "scope" of His will. A person is either in the will of God or they are out of His will. There is no middle ground. God does not operate in gray areas and that is exactly what "permissive will" is; a way for man to operate in a gray area, do what he finds most convenient, and feel good about his decision at the same time. Another way to define "permissive will" is by this one word: disobedience. Man will try to deify his disobedience and make himself appear holy by calling his disobedience by another name: God's permissive will. A person may assume that because God does not kill them or bring immediate harsh judgment upon them, then He must be pleased with their choice. No, God is simply displaying His grace and mercy, while at the same time, giving that person space to repent.

Thirdly, God bestowed man with a free will. He can make up his own mind as to a choice he wants to make. This writer thinks that what some call the "permissive will" of God is nothing more than man making up his own mind with his free will, deifying it by calling is by another name, and surviving by God's grace and mercy until repentance comes. And hopefully it will come because serious consequences follow when man leaves the "perfect" will of God and goes his own way. Remember, when one does not do the will of God, it is sin and sin always produces serious consequences. However, when one does the will of God then He prepares the way and provides for His own.

Finally, I summarize by saying that the "permissive will" does not exist. God does not wait to see what we are going to do in order to proclaim what His will is on a subject. Man fits into God's will. God does not fit into man's will. So, if a person decides to operate within the "permissive will" of God they are committing a sin and calling it by another name. Remember, a rose by any other name is still a rose and sin by any other name is still sin.

Chapter 3

Absolutes and Diversity

Galatians 1:6-10

I think it is necessary to establish the fact that there ARE absolutes and there is also such a thing as diversity. Absolutes are those things which cease to exist if they are blended in some way with diverse things. Truth is no longer truth when blended with a lie no matter how big or little it is. Moral conduct as defined by God is an absolute. When we go outside His definition then the conduct is immoral. Good is good and bad is bad. Black and white do exist even though man has always tried to color in shades of gray. God is God and there is no other. He is absolute. Jesus is the Savior and absolutely so. But, to the politically correct, the absolutes have to go. No one can get their feelings hurt or be excluded.

In this day and time, we hear a lot about diversity. In fact that word, diversity, is one of the favorite concepts of the politically correct who want to make sure that everyone is included and no one is left out. Another word for diversity is inclusiveness and we are led to believe that they are holy concepts when it comes to the formation of a society. At a meeting of liberal Baptists in Charlotte, N.C., the chair of the religion department of a major Baptist University said this, "Absolute truth claims are a warning sign of religion gone awry." The dean of that same university's religion department said this concerning Jesus, "Claims that Jesus Christ is the only way of salvation border on infringement of religious liberty." These two men are so diverse that they are in grave spiritual danger.

These two men are champions of diversity which is of the dangerous kind. Now, I do believe in diversity. I think it is great to be able to enjoy different things in life. I think that diversity in education is necessary if we are to have a functional society. I know that there is diversity in wealth as well as in political opinions. I am glad that there are blond, blue-eyed people and brown headed brown eyed people. I'm glad that some are short and some are tall. Some like some foods and others like different and diverse things. So, I do think diversity is a good thing. But when absolutes are compromised in order to have diversity, then diversity is not good. We can't be diverse on absolutes.

So, there are some absolutes from which we must not depart, for if we do, then eternal death awaits us. If we are to live, God has given us no options. We cannot be diverse. We must submit to His absolutes. This is where the world is going wrong and will miss partaking of the grace of God in Jesus Christ.

Chapter 4

Another Attack on Christianity

A few years ago there was a book and a movie of total fiction called *The Da Vinci Code*. The book was written by Dan Brown, the author of such books as *Digital Fortress*, *Angels and Demons* and *Deception Point*, and sold millions of copies. The movie by the same name was released shortly after the publication of the book. Both the book and movie are total fiction. They are meant to be fiction, but the world has picked up on it and they are ascribing truth to it for its substance. The great problem is that our spiritual enemy, Satan, has no problem clouding the minds of people to the point that they will accept these works of fiction as truth and at the same time reject the Word of God as the proper source. So we are in a spiritual battle which is manifesting itself in the debate over the *Da Vinci Code*. And, now we have this movie which is directed by Ron Howard (why, Opie wouldn't tell us anything wrong!) and starring Tom Hanks. The general public is so ignorant of spiritual things and also of the true facts about the *Da Vinci Code* that they will swallow the book and the movie and not even get spiritual heartburn. This sort of thing does untold damage to millions of souls who are led astray by it and who will be negatively influenced toward Jesus Christ and Christianity in general.

Now, I am not worried about the survival of Christianity or about the integrity of the Bible being compromised. I am certainly not worried about any damage this book and movie might do to the image of Jesus Christ. Christianity has withstood many, many such blows across the centuries and it is stronger today than ever. But, the question must be asked, Why should Christians and Christianity have to endure such a continuous onslaught? Dan Brown will come and go. The movie directed by Ron Howard will come and go. But, the Bible, Jesus and Christianity will continue to exist and get stronger. As a Christian, I am simply weary of a continual stream of attacks against our Lord Jesus Christ and God's Word. And, it is obvious that those who would believe the *Da Vinci Code*, in book or movie form, have no respect for what the Bible says. They would rather believe Dan Brown and Ron Howard than God's Word. There simply is no way to combat such ignorance. Jesus Christ who gave Himself for our sins should not be made a part of such irresponsible dribble as the *Da Vinci Code*.

I think this should be done: Christians should let their displeasure concerning the *Da Vinci Code* be known. Don't buy the book and ignore the movie. I am predicting that the movie will be a blockbuster because the world will be attracted to and adopt the false information and fiction contained in it as actual fact. Everyone likes a conspiracy and Dan Brown has dreamed up a very involved and contradictory one. Let me pose only one question: If, in the painting, *The Last Supper* by Leonardo Da Vinci, the person at the right hand of Jesus is not John but Mary Magdalene then where is John? He was the most beloved disciple. Is he then left out of the picture? There is so much more that needs to be refuted that it cannot be contained in this article but suffice it to say that one should not be tempted to believe this fictional book and they should not enrich those who would so treat Jesus by spending their money on *The Da Vinci Code*.

As Christians, we should be eternally grateful to God that He gave us the Bible and that we can have peace with Him if we only believe His Word. The world does not have that peace and therefore books and movies such as the *Da Vinci Code* appeals to them. Thank the Lord for the fact that our questions are answered in the eternal Word of God. We will be in a right relationship with God as long as we trust His Word and follow His instructions. We would do well to remember this: the way the world views Jesus Christ is not primarily dependent upon Hollywood and what they say or do. The world will formulate their feelings about Jesus by looking at His people and the way in which we follow Him.

Chapter 5

Cloning is Here!

Just as I and many others who watch world events closely have predicted, cloning of human beings is here. In a very short span of time cloning has progressed from simply talking about the possibilities to cloning sheep and other animals with the result that now the world is on the verge of seeing scientists clone human beings. The British and Italian scientists who are determined to go ahead with their efforts are simply not aware of the implications of doing such a thing. Of course they will always say that the creation of a "super race" is not their goal and that they decry such an effort, but nevertheless they continue with their experiments. Human nature being what it is, they should know that what they do in their world of scientific exploration will not stay in the lab very long. Mankind will exploit the ability to clone people and then, before one even knows it, the proverbial Pandora's Box will be opened with devastating results. There is now a cult which has stated that it will fund further scientific research and finally the cloning of humans with the idea of designing people who will be perfect for their purposes. They believe that they, themselves are cloned space aliens and that they must do the same kind of thing.

All of this points out the truth that anything man touches he always perverts. That has been true throughout human history. The old sin nature is destructive and, until redeemed, will always be drawn to the dark nature of things. All the rush to clone a human begs a question: If the scientists and doctors involved in this are not trying to create a "super human" who can be programmed a certain way and for certain purposes, then why are they doing all the research and developing the procedures for cloning humans? What is their purpose if not to be godlike themselves? I am aware of several things that cloning does which isn't mentioned very much. First, cloned animals grow old very rapidly and die sooner that their normal life span would be. Now why is that? It seems when cells from older animals are used for the cloning that the newly produced animal inherits the genetic "time line" of the older cells. So, when they are born their body cells are programmed with a lot of time already consumed which means that at the time of birth their cell structure is already as old as the animal which donated the genetic materials. Secondly, while the successful efforts at cloning are highly publicized, the failure rate is extremely high. Included in those failures are those which did not produce a living clone and those which produced a grotesquely malformed clone. What will scientists and doctors do with human clones which are grotesque in nature? They will simply do away with them. If by abortion they will destroy a normal human baby who was created by God, then why not destroy something created by them which did not measure up to their scientific standards? The genie is out of the bottle where cloning is concerned and there is no telling what kind of destructive things that genie will do.

Another aspect of a cloned human which I have not heard discussed is this: Will it have a soul and a spirit? Of course, I do not expect the secular world and the scientists to think about such a spiritual thing, but the implications are enormous. I believe that only God can bestow a soul and spirit to an individual. Man might engineer a living organism, but he will never be able to instill a spirit and soul in that organism. So, then what might happen? It would be possible for a government to create an army of people who would do their bidding with no soul or spirit with which to be guided. Those who engineered them would be their conscience and god. They would make brutal soldiers who have no conscience. They could become despots which would be more wicked than anything mankind has seen so far in the history of the world. I also think, as I read the prophetic scriptures about the end of time, that an engineered human would make the perfect antichrist who would be completely under satanic control. I think this is a feasible thing to consider. And, I am convinced that this cloning technology is not coming on the scene at this present time in history by simple chance. I think it has implications for the end times.

If the scientific community is successful in reproducing humans by cloning, we are faced with the most serious situation concerning human history that we have ever faced. Remember, that unsaved human beings are not indwelt by the Spirit of God and they will always have a tendency to go toward the "dark". They will not, by nature, desire to do the things of God and they will, by nature, dishonor whatever is of God. It is dangerous thing that is happening today with the scientific world—which nearly always denies God for their belief in evolution—to having their hands on the ability to clone humans.

Make no mistake about it, our own government is already involved with this scientific venture and will eventually lower the barriers and delve into cloning themselves. I think we should let our congressmen know that we do not want them to take part in authorizing this kind of procedure. God will not long allow man to go in this direction without His judgment falling upon us. We are on dangerous ground and we must not go any further.

Chapter 6

Confused, Convoluted Christianity

When Satan was banished from heaven and cast down to the earth, he did not cease his destructive work. In fact it was just beginning. He "turned up the heat."

He did not see himself as having been "retired" from heaven. His view was that he had simply changed jobs and the location of his work. His area of influence was reduced. While in heaven, he had heaven-wide influence because of who he was and where he was serving. After he was kicked out of heaven his job changed and his area of influence was smaller ... earth. But that has not deterred him at all and he has been very successful in his attempts to do damage to God's creation and to His people.

The Church and Christians are major areas of Satan's concentration. He is smart enough to know that the church will be around forever so he knows he can't destroy it. So, one of his tactics is to so corrupt the beliefs of even those who claim Christ that many unsaved would be led astray into an eternal hell. I can hear him now, "If I corrupt those who are a part of the church then I can use them to deceive others because people will tend to trust them and the church of which they are a part."

How much has he been successful at this ploy? What ridiculous and unbiblical things do people within the scope of Christianity now accept and, using their trusted influence, lead others to accept?

Before our age of cultured diversity and before worldwide travel became an everyday thing, our cherished Christian doctrines were not so harshly questioned or under such constant and strenuous attack. But, in this day of cultural diversity we are discovering just how easy it is for Christianity to be corrupted by being blended with pagan religions from foreign lands. In addition, Bible doubting liberals within Christianity are continuing their destructive ways. One would hope that our Christian people would be so well grounded that they would be impervious to a shift in beliefs, but, we are finding out that this is not the case.

With all that is happening, we must make sure that we teach our children that which is doctrinally correct. They are easily influenced during the early years and we must make sure that they don't grow up confused. While the world under Satan's influence demands that we not teach our children our cherished beliefs concerning God's work of salvation, the world stands ready to move in and deposit its damnable doctrines in their hearts poisoning them in the most deadly of ways. The first lie goes something like this, "Don't violate the personal freedoms of your children to make up their own minds." We must remember that the Word of God instructs us to teach our children our religious beliefs so that they will have the proper foundation in life. This is exactly what Satan does not want. He does not want a person to have a life founded upon the proper things. He wants a mind which is unsure and wavering. He works most effectively with a mind that is open to any and every lie simply because it knows so little that anything it hears is quickly absorbed as truth.

We, as faithful servants of the Lord, must make it our goal to teach the proper doctrines and live by those doctrines to the extent that we are a living testimony to the saving power of God through Jesus Christ.

Confused, Convoluted Christianity

One of the biggest lies which has been perpetuated upon the church is the idea that if we lower our standards just a little then we will be able to minister to them and get them saved. The only problem with that is that it won't work. Many churches are giving the world its desires in music, dress, activities and doctrine in order to be at the top of the heap when it comes to looking at statistics and money. The driving force in many of today's churches is numbers and money and both of those things should not be at the core of who we are and what we do.

If we tell the people of the world who are in need of salvation that we will lower the bar so that it will be easy to step over it to come to our church then they will be more than happy to come. If we tell them that they don't have to change their dress, music, level of dedication or make a public confession of faith then they will step right over that low bar and walk right in. They don't have to change a thing; just come. The holiness of worship is then sacrificed on the altar of personal preferences especially in music and dress. I was talking recently with a young preacher who has bitten the bait. As I tried to reason with him on this issue, he said, "Well, we don't compromise the preaching of the Word." My immediate response was, "So you are saying that you *do* compromise everything else but just not the Word." He didn't quite know how to respond but needless to say, his answer lacked a lot. What many today do not understand is that the method and mode will determine the message to a great extent. The environment will set the expectations for what is to take place and in such a situation, people will allow the environment to determine just how they approach the preaching of the Word. It doesn't matter if the preacher is trying to be faithful at that point, the environment he has created in order to get the world to come will hinder a proper respect for the proclamation of the Word.

When I think about the day that Jesus Christ died on the Cross of Calvary, and when I think about the serious nature of what He was accomplishing on the cross, I am reminded of the fact that we should conduct ourselves with the same kind of gravity and seriousness which His death on the cross exhibits for us. When Christians come together, their primary function should be to worship. Discipleship is a close second, but worship is the primary function for which we were created.

The early church came together to worship and learn. Much of what the church is doing today has very little to do with our primary function as the Body of Christ. It has a lot to do with social interaction, fun and fellowship. I know that we live in a modern day and that many things are going to be different, but the essence of who we are and what we are should never change because who and what we are is based on an unchangeable fact; Jesus died for our sins. Whoever said that just because we live in a different day that so much of the world should be accepted by the church as normal Christian behavior?

Evangelism does no more than extend religion. It seeks to enlarge, but often there is little thought given to quality instead of quantity. Present-day evangelism accepts the present-day form of Christianity as the same as in the Apostles' day, and it gets busy about converting people to that present-day form. I would submit that our present day Christianity is quite different from the Christianity of Paul's day. Present-day evangelism asks few questions about what a person thinks they are being converted to.

When we talk about evangelism, we need to ask this question, "Evangelize them to what?" If we are going to evangelize them to much of what we have, and are becoming, then we will be leading them astray. We should not evangelize someone to an *easy-believism* and social Christianity. Too often people are being led to believe that, "if you'll repent to some extent, you'll be saved to some degree." That kind of repentance will get a person nowhere with God. We should not lead them to identify with a watered down Gospel which must always be fun, fulfilling and non-confronting to sin. The reason we should not do this is that we would be evangelizing them to something Christianity is not. If we are going to witness and evangelize people it must be to the genuine thing.

Confused, Convoluted Christianity

Many churches of today are experiencing a lot of trouble and disruption because they have invited the world inside. It has been all too willing to come because they gather that if they come to church, sing and listen to a sermon, they are going to go to heaven when they die. They are looking for the least common denominator of spiritual "safety" and they think they have found it. When the world comes into the church it brings its ideas and approaches which will not work in a Godly environment. Modern day Christianity is confused and convoluted because it is looking to the world's methods to build the church and that will never work. Christianity is supposed to be different from the world but we now think that the way to win it is to be like it.

So, as one can see, Satan is attacking us from the inside. He, knowing human nature, is confident that we will allow ourselves to be corrupted on the inside so we can look good on the outside.

Chapter 7

In Trouble

Since retiring from the active pastorate on July 31st, 2012, I have been preaching in many different and varied places. It has been a real joy to be able to be among the people of God in various churches. It is truly a blessing to be able to minister to people by preaching God's Word to them. I have been impressed by how many good, godly people are members of our churches, especially the smaller ones.

I am encouraged by the great Christian people I have met, I am also concerned by what I see and hear in many churches. While I hate to say it, I think that based on what takes place in the vast majority of our churches, Christianity is being weakened and its churches are in trouble. I know that the church will survive until the coming of Jesus but I am afraid that it is growing weaker by the day. It is not in trouble based on its beliefs and doctrines. They are sound and secure even though the world is trying to alter these as well. But, the church is in trouble because she is basically doing nothing, based on my observations as I travel around and preach. This is not a new revelation to me, but it has been confirmed as I have been exposed to different congregations. I have often said that I do not understand why the people keep coming back each Sunday with no more enthusiasm and energy than is being experienced in our churches. To put it bluntly; they are dead, dead, dead. There is no excitement and energy about being in God's house on His day. When the preacher takes the pulpit to bring God's Word, he has to generate any energy that is in the room in order to be able to preach with enthusiasm and power. It should not be left up to the preacher to generate the energy in the worship service. He should find the people energized and expectant to hear what the Lord has to say.

Note also, Sunday School is not functional because of a lack of organization and teachers who are unprepared to teach the lesson. Discussions tend to be centered on topics which have nothing to do with the purpose for coming to church. So, how can we expect the people to be committed to Sunday School if the main topic, the Bible lesson, is not given proper consideration while football, hunting, fishing, family and professional careers are fully discussed? As I was waiting to preach in one church, I happened to look down and observed a folder laying on the front pew. It was rosy pink in color and written on the front of it in bold Marks-A-Lot print were the words, "Sunday School Stuff." I think that explains why many don't want to come to Bible Study. If it has no more priority than being referred to as "stuff" then there is a serious problem.

In addition to the things discussed above, I believe that the main problem in many of our churches is related to the Pastor. The people in the pew know very little doctrine and are spiritually immature because they are not being equipped to live a dynamic Christian life, much less to be a part of a church which functions properly. The primary work of the ministry is to be found in the preaching of the Word. Churches will properly function in direct proportion to the level of Biblical preaching they experience. A pastor must spend the proper amount of time studying and preparing to preach. His primary function is not to be found in counseling. It is not in visiting the sick. It is not in eating crumpets with the little ladies and having coffee with the boys. His primary function is to be found in preaching. If he is not willing to spend the proper time to prepare a sermon which is informative, inspiring, interesting and edifying, then he should find himself something else to do. I believe that if God calls a man to preach then that should be his focus. Visiting the sick and other pastoral duties must also be done but they should not be an excuse for not having enough time to prepare to preach. The people in the vast majority of our churches are being cheated out of a deeper and more dynamic relationship to the Lord because the sermons they are hearing are "sermonettes for Christianettes." They are empty, vapid, and insipid. They are not the "meat" Paul speaks about but they are nothing more than the "foam" on a latte. When God calls one to a particular task then He equips the person to perform that task. Everyone has talents to a different extent, but everyone called to preach should give it his best so that God can speak through him and edify His saints.

I recently asked two different churches if they knew the definition of expository preaching. Only one man in one of the churches raised his hand. Two congregations, gathered for Sunday morning worship, could not tell me what expositional preaching is. They said that as far as they knew, they had never heard an expository sermon. They did not know what it is supposed to seek to accomplish. They were ignorant of the term, expository preaching. Most of these people have been in church for thirty years or more. These people knew very little doctrine but they absorbed it like a sponge. Suddenly the Bible became clear to them. They loved to learn the deeper truths contained in a passage. Expository preaching is work. It does not come easily as one has to do extensive word studies and research. It is the work of the ministry that God has for everyone He has called to be a preacher. Teaching the people the doctrines of the Bible will solve most of their problems. The more they learn the more peace and prosperity they will experience. The little problems that trouble most churches will vanish as the people learn the doctrines which apply to various situations. Expository, doctrinal preaching cannot be replaced and should be the focus of the pastor.

We are In Trouble in our churches today primarily because the people have not been taught the Bible from the pulpit as they should have been. In addition to this, the majority of preachers today are afraid to tell the people many things they need to know in order to keep them properly informed. They are too afraid of the ACLU, the IRS and Americans United for the Separation of Church and State. Preachers today have been "muffled" very effectively because of the threat of law suits or the loss of the church's tax exempt status. Political correctness has silenced the one person in society which should be warning the people about things they are dealing with. The only place in our society which does not have total freedom of speech is the one place that should be totally free and that is the pulpit. Preachers are being held hostage at the price of the tax monies they fear they might lose if they speak on certain issues. Obedience is being extorted from them under the threat of losing their tax exempt status. If the preachers knew the law and understood the freedoms they actually possess then they would discover that they can do and say much more than they have, so far, been willing to do. In essence, God's spokesmen are being cowered into a corner for the sake of a little tax money. This should not be.

So, I observe that the reason for so many weak churches is to be found in the failure of the pulpit to preach the Word to the best of the preacher's ability and the failure to lead their people with enthusiasm and energy. People will do far more than they are being asked to do. My philosophy is that we should ask them to do things. The only thing they can say is "no" and if they do give a negative answer then the pastor is no worse off. Plus, he can't be accused of not trying to lead his people. Most churches today are doing nothing. The people have to be either very, very dedicated or totally habited to keep showing up every Sunday. My observation is that most are totally habited. They are going through the motions in order to do what they think is right before God. They are good people who want to please God but they are accomplishing very little and reaching almost no one with the Gospel.

Sadly, most of our churches are not doing much more than existing. They possess very little that would make a person decide that they would like to be a member. It doesn't take hype, loud secular sounding music, popular little choruses and modern innovation to make a person decide they would like to identify with a particular church. It takes solid Biblical preaching, serious study of the Word, a functioning outreach program, good well-grounded music which is presented in a sincere and well performed manner. The music should not sound like "a dying calf in a hailstorm."

If a church would do these things well, then the Lord will be able to bless them and grow them as He desires.

Many of the churches I have seen are within only a few years of closing their doors unless something is done to revitalize them. Most are filled with members who are in their last decade of life. A lot of these churches have only thirty people or so. Within five to ten years they will cease to exist. Our Southern Baptist Convention is loaded with the kind of churches I have described in this piece. It is sad. We are In Trouble.

Chapter 8

Islam and Government

If our leaders made one grave mistake when they decided to engage a Muslim nation in a war, it was that there was no one advising the President who understood the Muslim religion and some of the implications of becoming involved with them. This writer is certainly no expert on this major world religion either but one thing is glaringly evident about those nations which hold to Islam: they see their religion and government as the same thing.

One will remember that when the U.S. went to war with Iraq right after the world trade center bombing, the people of Iraq and other Muslim countries immediately said that we were warring against Islam. Our leaders quickly responded that we were not warring against Islam but against those who attacked our country. What our leaders failed to see is that in the minds of those people we attacked Islam when we attacked their government because in their minds and tradition, they are the same thing. In America we do not equate our religion with our government. We would like for our government to display Christian characteristics but we do not say that our government and our Christian religion are the same. We allow for freedom of religion and our government stands apart from that in an official way. America was founded by

Christians and has been identified as a Christian nation, but we do not say that Christianity is tantamount to our government.

This is a major point of difficulty in our country at present. When Hindu people come to America we allow them freedom of religion but they do not establish a government founded upon and the same as the Hindu religion or a Hindu nation. When Buddhists come here they have freedom of worship but they do not come here with the idea of establishing a government which is seen as the same thing as Buddhism. But when the Muslims come to America and take advantage of our freedom of religion, we need to understand that, in their minds, we are also giving them the freedom of government. Our leaders need to understand that the Muslim people understand that they are bringing their government to our shores because they view their religion (Islam) and their government as one and the same. *We are offering freedom of religion but not freedom of government and that needs to be addressed.* If it is not addressed then what we have allowed is the transfer of another governmental nation and legal system within our own borders. This is true of no one else, but to the Muslims it is a fact.

Our "weakness" at this point is our willingness to allow freedom of religion. In fact, our constitution guarantees that the government will not become involved in the establishment of a religion or in the denying of the practice of one's religion. Others take advantage of this situation to our own demise. We cannot have two governments with vastly differing legal systems operating in the same borders. In some places such as Dearborn, Michigan the Muslim influence is changing the government of the city and area. Dearborn, Michigan has the second largest concentration of Muslims outside of the Middle East and they demand that they be allowed to govern themselves. They demand that Sharia Law be allowed. We have sadly heard of "honor killings" which is allowed under Sharia Law. We have never seen anything like this in America before. The city of Paris, France has a huge concentration of Muslims. They have established their own areas of Paris in which to live. They are also allowed to practice Sharia Law apart from the laws of France. London has the same situation with the British government allowing the Muslims to practice their own kind of law apart from Britain's legal system. This is where it is headed in America unless something is done to avert it. Certain concentrations of Muslims will become so predominant that they will demand our legal system be set aside for their system which is grounded in their own government ... Islam. At that point we cease to be a sovereign nation.

This article is a warning to our leaders who do not seem to understand that many Muslims have come here with their own governmental system of laws to which they are more loyal than they are to our laws. They are more loyal to their legal system because it is founded in their religion to which they are strongly dedicated. And being founded in Islam also means that it is their government which they have brought with them because they see their government and religion as one and the same. All of this demands from us an eternal vigilance to make sure that our sovereignty as a nation is not compromised by anyone. We must have leaders who, under the harshest of pressure, will stand totally committed to the Constitution of the United States of America. While we can guarantee people freedom of religion, we cannot allow them freedom of their government which is seen by them as tantamount to their religion practiced so freely in the United States.

There is an old saying which says, "When in Rome do as the Romans do.' This means that you are to forget about your laws and social mores and subject yourself to the laws and way of life of the "Romans." But the Muslims say. "When in Rome do as the Muslims do." Or, paraphrased, "When in America do as the Muslims do."

This is a dangerous situation and if it were the Hindus, Buddhists or anyone else, we would say the same thing.

Chapter 9

Living in the Overload Zone

With all of the trouble we have in the world today, do you find that you function somewhere in the "overload" zone in your life? In years gone by the public was not bombarded by all of the tragedies and troubles of the world on a moment by moment basis. If something took place which was particularly troubling, most people would not find out about it until the event was at least two or three days old. Of course, the closer it came to home, the quicker the news traveled; but most world news then was what today's mainstream media dubs as "old news" by the time we got it. By then one would reason that since it was a few days old and since it had exerted no impact upon their lives that they were safe from it and therefore did not worry about it. But today it is different. News organizations such as CNN, FOX, MSNBC and the major networks make sure that everyone in the world has the ability to consume any and all types of news immediately. If there is a bombing in Israel (something you can do nothing about) you know it before the smoke clears. If there is a murder which is particularly gruesome, you know it before the blood stains dry. If there is a natural disaster it is as if it is taking place in your own living room. If there are starving children anywhere in the world, you are transported right into their midst. And, the average person feels the frustration, pain and guilt of not being able to do anything about all of this.

So, the question arises; just what is news to me and when is a happening turned into a production so that the news media can sell commercials and be the one who can claim that they were "the first to bring you the story." Personally, I feel that real news is anything that has a direct bearing on my life and the lives of my family members. These are the things that I need to know about and news should be something you *need* to know not something that is mere information.

Furthermore, the real news is made up of bare facts minus all of the commentary that is espoused by so many of the news personalities today. I believe that one reason so many people live with so much tension and frustration is that they are continually confronted with things they cannot control and can do nothing about. Being the good people they are, and desiring to help people, they find themselves under undue stress because the news media has told them *information* which is beyond their ability to affect in any way. Just think about it this way. The next time you view the news just ask these questions following each story, "Now, did I *need* to know that?" "How does that affect me personally?" If you cannot find a valid reason why you needed to be exposed to the information then it was not news to you, but simply information. Then determine in yourself that you will not let those things which are hurled at you each evening stir you into fits of guilt and frustration because of your inability to do something about them. Don't let the information raise your blood pressure and cause fits of anxiety.

I recently told a person who was giving me material to read that I had so much stuff I *had* to read that I didn't have time to read some things I *wanted* to read. I feel the same about the news and what is fed to us. I spend so much time dealing with things I *have* to deal with in ordinary life that I don't have time to spend on things I can do nothing about. But I want to share with you that I have discovered how to take the tension out of life and to live above the things going on around me. The only person who has the answers to life is Jesus Christ. When I committed my life to Him and He became my Savior, I found that His Spirit led me to believe *everything* He says in the Bible.

In Matthew 6:25 and following, Jesus talks about our trust in God and how we should not worry. He says in verse 33, "But seek ye first the kingdom of God and all these things shall be added unto you." I believe in a Sovereign God who knows everything and who is in control of His universe. He cannot be caught by surprise (because that would indicate that He thought something else was going to happen and therefore He is not omniscient), and you cannot disappoint Him (disappointment would indicate that he expected something else and was disappointed when it didn't take place. This would indicate that He was not sovereign and could not control the events of life.) When I believe in a Sovereign God, I relieve myself from the frustration, worry, high blood pressure and tensions of life. It makes life much sweeter. It also helps one decide what really is important and how they should react to it.

So the next time things start pushing you into the "Overload Zone" just remember that it was never designed by God for you to live that way. Also remember that He *is* in control no matter what the circumstances are saying to you. The God who is able to handle anything and everything did not intend for us to live in the "Overload Zone."

Chapter 10

Mirroring the Gravity of the Cross

There are some places to which one goes that command respect. For instance, when one goes to our National Cemetery at Arlington, Virginia, there is a certain amount of respect which is demanded. In the courtrooms of America respect for the judge and the rule of law is required. If a person were to visit the White House, they would be held to strict rules governing their conduct and access to the building. When someone goes to a funeral to pay their last respects to an individual, they dress and act accordingly. If one were called to the Mayor's office or to the office of a high government official, they would feel obligated to honor the person holding that office by treating them with respect. And so, my point is made that certain places to which one goes command respect. This attitude of respect will affect one's dress and conduct. It will keep them soberly aware of where they are and who it is that they are dealing with. It will also have a lot to do with their activities while they are in this place which commands respect.

In the world in which we now live, people have respect for just about anyone, anything and any place more than they have respect for the Lord's House and what is being done there. I think that we should always bear in mind that what we do in worship should always mirror the gravity of what was done on the cross for us. But many have forgotten that idea. The Lord's House is now treated with no more respect that a soccer field or a gymnasium by some people. It is no longer a place for a worshipful experience which mirrors the gravity of the cross, but it is a place of entertainment which gratifies the flesh and the warm fuzzy feelings of the people in attendance. It is supposed to be a place of fun, and if it is not then something must obviously be missing.

It is a sign of our age that worship, in many churches, has turned into nothing more than entertainment. And, along with this attitude we find that the respect for the place is also decreasing at a quantum pace. That is why people feel comfortable in going to a "worship" service dressed as they would go to a soccer game or a gym. That's why children are not taught to display your best for the Lord, but that anything goes. They are allowed to go to church in their worst instead of their best. When I was a child I was taught to always present your best to the Lord. Some had more than others, but that did not keep us from presenting our best. Why? Because we were going to a special place which demanded respect to worship our wonderful Lord who commanded respect.

The breaking down of the barriers of what is expected when we enter the Lord's House as well as what we do while we are there is a serious threat to Christianity. In fact, I think that we now have too loose a definition of what worship is. Remember, what we do in our worship must mirror the gravity of what took place on the cross. If we do not do that then we dishonor what the Lord did there. This idea of loosening things up so that the world will not be "offended" by our worship and therefore will come to our churches is the wrong method. So they are told, "Come as you are and we will show you a church service which will allow you to do just about as you please." The respect for the place and for the purpose of their being there is lost. The respect for the Lord is diminished because He becomes someone who does not command respect in their eyes. People are basically being taught that He is no one special and that the Gospel makes no demands on the life.

Mirroring the Gravity of the Cross

The world system is a doomed system. Christianity cannot succeed by buying into a doomed system. We must never mold Christianity into the image of the world in order to try to save the world. It will not work. We must never employ worldly methods in the church in order to simply gain numbers. And, make no mistake about it, most of what many are doing today is grounded in a passionate desire for numbers and money. "Give them what they want and they will come" is the theory.

I think we must remember this from the Bible. One day a large crowd of people were following Jesus. They were watching Him do the miracles and they loved it They were listening to His sermon and they loved it. They were having a great time fellowshipping with the others in the crowd and they loved it. They were following a miracle worker and a prophet and they loved it. Everyone was happy and they all felt that they were having a wonderful experience with God. They felt good about themselves. But, then, Jesus turned to the crowd and began to tell them what the kingdom was all about and what would be expected of them, many of them left Him. In fact, he turned to His disciples and said "Will ye also go away"? Then Simon Peter said, "Lord, to whom shall we go? Thou hast the words of eternal life." As long as it seemed easy, rational and the popular thing to do, they followed Jesus, but when He showed the crowd the gravity of the Christian life they left. While it was easy, enlightening and non-committal they were willing to stay, but when they were brought into the light of the reality of the Christian life, they left. So, when the real truth about Jesus and the Kingdom dawned upon them, it thinned out the crowd. Remember, a crowd is not the goal. Honoring God in true worship which mirrors the gravity of the Lord's work on the cross is the true goal. And, in the process the Gospel is preached which will offend the heart of the unbeliever according to scripture. But, under the guidance of the Holy Spirit, those who will be saved will repent of their sins and turn to the Lord for salvation. And that's the work of the Holy Spirit and not of man.

Yes a cheapening of the Gospel and a cheapening of true worship is taking place. It is a dangerous thing for those who are being fooled by it. Our respect for the place of worship is diminishing and it is breeding a disrespect for the Gospel being preached. As long as it is fun and popular people will flock to it and we would expect the world to react to it in that way. We must treat the Lord with the highest respect. We must treat His House with the same respect. We must conduct ourselves with an attitude of respect when we worship Him and we must display that respect in what we do.

Strange things are happening today and those who get too loose and go too far will live to regret it.

Chapter 11

Perseverance or Preservation?

Recently while in a discussion about the pervasive influence of Calvinism in our Southern Baptist Zion, I was struck by the fact that one individual used the term Preservation when referring to the fifth point of that theological model. I had noticed that others also made this mistake and didn't seem to notice the error. In a very subtle way I brought the error to the writer's attention and he was most grateful for the fact that I had done so. Some might ask why get so picky about such a thing? Everyone knows what my friend was referring to and trying to say.

Not so quick. There is a world of difference between perseverance and preservation and we cannot confuse the two. The central core of the difference is that perseverance is a *man* work and preservation is a *God* work. One is earthly and the other is heavenly. One is a work and the other is a gift. One, man can do and the other only God can perform.

If a person is a dyed-in-the-wool Five Point Calvinist he cannot give a positive answer when asked if he knows whether he is saved or not. The simple fact of the matter is that his theological model does not afford him the assurance of salvation so he is clinging to perseverance and hoping that he is one of the elect.

Some day they will know if they persevered to the point that they were acceptable to God but in the meantime they cannot say for sure if they made the grade or not. So, they have to die to find out if they were saved. They cannot know for sure that they are a saved person? John says in 1 John 5:13, "These things have I written unto you that believe on the name of the Son of God that ye may know that ye have eternal life, and that ye may believe on the name of the Son of God." Why would John say such a thing unless one can know for sure that they are a saved person? John is speaking from the perspective of assurance brought by God's promise of preservation and the Calvinist is speaking from the perspective of perseverance which man must accomplish himself.

The problem with perseverance is that it is relative. Who is to say when one has reached the point of proving their salvation and being acceptable to God? When is God satisfied? One might say that going to church, tithing their income and providing a good living for their family is enough. Another would say that living a good life, not using profanity, giving to missions, reading the Bible and showing mercy is what it will take to prove their salvation by perseverance. Even another might say that forty years of perfect Sunday School attendance would prove they were a genuine Christian. The point is made that perseverance is relative. What suffices for one is not enough for another. That is because it is a man work and must satisfy a man's point of view whatever that point of view might be.

When one is to persevere in any endeavor it is meant that they will strive and work until they finish the job. It is a work viewpoint of proving salvation. That is why many Calvinists will say, "I am hoping" instead of "I know." They live in the world of wondering when or if they have done enough to please God. At what point did they achieve that magic level of achievement which will assure them of eternal life with God? The problem is that perseverance is a *man* work and man cannot assure himself of heaven.

Perseverance or Preservation?

Preservation is something quite different. Man cannot preserve himself. It must be done by someone else and God is quite clear that He is the one who finishes the good work in us, not we ourselves. Those who give their lives to Jesus in simple faith and commit their lives to Him in repentance receive the promise given in Romans 10:9-10. He can have assurance of his salvation and know of his saving relationship to God because he trusts Jesus to do all that is needed to save him and he doesn't have to do anything himself. Jesus provided all that was needed when he died on the cross and was resurrected for our justification. I rest in Him and not in my ability to prove anything; I certainly don't need to prove that I am a genuine Christian. My life of obedience is the best evidence of true salvation having taken place in me. The fruits of a life that is in a redemptive relationship with Jesus Christ is evidence of true salvation as Jesus tells us in John 15. But, those fruits are a by-product produced in my life by the indwelling Holy Spirit and not fruits produced by me as I persevere to the end. Actually these fruits become works if they are a part of my persevering. They are fruits when trusting Jesus and the validity of His promises are the foundation for my assurance of salvation. So, when Jesus' promises prove my salvation as I trust in them, I will show evidence as fruits emerge from my life by His power. When He does it, it is fruits. When man strives to persevere it results in works.

This could go on and on but the New Testament, and particularly the writings of Paul are replete with the truth of what I am saying. Anyone with even a modicum of familiarity with Paul's writings knows that assurance was one of the hallmarks of his faith in Christ. And they will also know that he rested in the unfailing promises of God concerning salvation. God produces the evidence when He has worked salvation in a person through their personal belief in and commitment to Jesus for salvation. Man produces works when he has something to prove and is hoping that he persevered enough to get into heaven when he dies.

To reiterate and summarize. Preservation is a God work; Perseverance is a man work. That makes the salvation of one who is persevering a works salvation. One who is preserved is preserved by their saving relationship to Jesus Christ which is grounded upon His promises to us when we trust in Him.

Chapter 12

The Abuse of Heaven

On Tuesday evening, December 20, 2005, I witnessed one of the greatest abuses I have ever seen. The ABC television network aired a "special" by none other than that great icon of spirituality, Barbara Walters. When I saw the promos aired concerning this program I knew immediately that the American public would be led astray in one of the most important of matters. The American media giants have never been able to get it right when they are dealing with spiritual matters, especially Christianity. It is absolutely beyond me how anyone could so consistently be so wrong in what they say about religion and religious matters. It would have to be intentional for people to be so blatantly wrong so much of the time. Well, Barbara Walters and her special on heaven gets the prize. She should be nominated for the "Abuse of Heaven" award. The program was atrocious. It was incorrect and misleading. It was downright heretical in its content. And, to top it off, it led the evening in ratings of all networks.

The sad thing is that many people in society are honestly searching for the answers to some very important questions concerning life, death and the afterlife. They are hungry for any information they can find. Well, Barbara Walters gave them plenty of information but the only problem is that ninety-eight percent of it was wrong. About the only thing that was correct was the fact that there *is* a heaven. And, there was even some doubt about that in the minds of some of those interviewed. No matter who Ms. Walters was interviewing she seemed to accept the fact that everyone had a view which was correct in some way. The real problem was that she has no foundation herself for a correct Biblical understanding of heaven. To her, it is a place where people from many different religions go in some way to some place. The only thing they can agree upon is that it is a good place where they no longer have to struggle with the trials of life.

If one listened even casually, they would conclude that the name of the program should have been "Heaven, Have It Your Way". Of course I don't know what people would expect from a person like Ms. Walters who is Jewish by birth but who has never practiced her religion. She just "never got into it" as she said. And one wonders why in the world would the ABC television network assign such a person to deal with such an important topic? The sad thing is that human beings will absorb the incorrect information contained in the program far quicker than they will absorb what God says about the issue of heaven or anything else for that matter.

Even sadder is the fact that all the preachers in America preaching every Sunday for the next year on Heaven would not counteract the damage done by Barbara Walters' program. The primary reason for this fact is that we would be "preaching to the choir" on the issue. The people who go to church regularly already have a correct view of Heaven while millions who are searching for answers watched and absorbed the incorrect information dispensed by Ms. Walters. The program led the evening in viewers which tells you that people are really searching. Sadly, and tragically they looked to the wrong source for information.

Chapter 13

The Firewall

The only thing which is standing in the way of the secular society taking over completely is the Bible and those who preach and believe it.

Just what would be taking place if the Bible did not stand in their way?

Satan has always known that this would be the case and that is why he always casts doubt on the Word of God. He started in the garden with, "Yea, did God really say … ?" He has inspired the formation of thousands of cults each of which have their own written "scriptures" which are designed to validate the thoughts of the cult leader or leaders. Satan always starts by casting doubt on God's Word since it is the foundation of all that is godly and holy. It is our instruction book on how to get to heaven and live a Godly life here on earth. So, Satan attacks it seeking to destroy our argument against him and his wickedness. A problem arises when we realize that the average person knows so little about their "foundation" that they are an easy victim of anyone who wants to tell them anything that is in error concerning God, His Word and His Work especially through Jesus Christ.

The world always criticizes the church for talking about certain sins to the exclusion of others … homosexuality, same sex marriage … abortion … drunkenness. But, it is the secularist that keeps pushing those themes. They bring them up and then condemn the church for doing battle against them. They define the battleground and then condemn us for fighting on it! The church isn't running to and fro picking an argument over particular sins. We realize that any sin which is unforgiven causes a valid separation from God unless it is redeemed. So, the battlefield is defined by those pushing their agenda and the attack is launched against the church and God's Word from that particular angle. We find ourselves standing against sin in an environment we did not define and it is very easy for Satan to make the world believe that we, the church, started the whole battle. We are, as Luther said, "Captive" to the Word. We have no choice but to stand for what it says since it is our foundation.

But many find that it is more convenient and expedient to abandon their foundation in order to appear not so critical. They have also accepted the idea that they formulated the battle and started the fight because of their convictions. Remember, Satan's crowd will define the battleground and then condemn us for fighting on it. When a church, denomination or individual abandons their foundation (God's Word) then they will not last long. They will fade away into oblivion sooner or later. Several denominations are in this decline right now because they have compromised their foundation and will eventually die.

The church, God's people, is the only institution which is condemned because it is founded upon and refers to the Bible as its source book. That is why the church is so castigated and condemned. It is founded upon that which Satan most wants to destroy. The secularist, humanist, atheist and infidel liberals of society want to live unrestrained lives, and the church, founded upon the Bible, is standing in the way. We are the only organization that makes them feel constrained. An open, liberal society doesn't want anything to constrain it in any way and therefore they seek to discredit the church in order to excuse their own actions.

The Firewall

It is the church and the Bible which are preserving some sense of sanity in society. We are the only ones who have the desire or the authority or the power inherent in God's Word to do this battle and we must stand up to it. God's people must never make an excuse for what they believe if it is founded upon the Word. Too many preachers today are reticent to say what they know is right because of a fear of offending society. Just remember, society is easily offended if they think that it will make the church look guilty of something. And, the church has bitten the bait in that it is afraid that if it stands for what our foundation demands, we will certainly be guilty of offending. One thing one must not do in this present day world is offend anyone. Offending someone has become the modern day "capital crime." We must realize that if one is offended by the truth, then so be it. They are guilty of putting themselves in that position and the church didn't put them there. But, we are bound by the Word to proclaim what God says and not what man says.

We need, no, we must have more preachers who will be willing to stand and proclaim that which is godly and right, not what they think the world will digest. Many preachers have become experts at "almost saying something." The reason they are adept at that approach is that they want to sound brave but at the same time keep from offending those who hold a view which is against the Bible. One must say what God says and let the "chips fall where they may." We need to have a new generation of preachers who will not be afraid to give our sinful secular society a good case of heartburn without then quickly turning and offering them some watered down antacid so they won't be mad at us. A true preacher must say what he says, mean what he says and then stand on it no matter what!

If we are to be the Firewall that stands for righteousness and confront in a sinful society, then we must start acting differently because the church is quickly being absorbed into the world while running with open arms toward it forever seeking acceptance.

So, as stated above, the church is the only organization (organism) that is standing in the way of the complete and utter breakdown of society. We possess what the world needs to survive, and we must not be reticent about stating who we are and standing for it.

Chapter 14

The Implications of Obedience

"If you love me, keep my commandments."—John 14:15

When the average person thinks about obedience, they automatically calculate that it means that one should do what they are told. While that is absolutely right, there is much more to the situation and we should be aware of what that word, obedience implies.

Obedience, in and of itself, is a concept which means nothing if there is no choice involved. Obedience without a choice loses its meaning altogether. Obedience without a choice is not obedience, it is rote conformity without even knowing why one has done something or the implications of it.

Our passage of Scripture unites obedience with a powerful concept, love. If one obeys, they should do so because they love that person or entity which has desired obedience from them. I should obey the Lord because I love him, not because I fear him or because He has designed me to obey him in a rote manner and fall into line on any issue. His love for me and mine for Him should lead me to seek to please Him and therefore follow His commandments in humble obedience.

Now, we have hit on another concept which is vitally involved, and that is humility. True obedience will never issue forth from a person or entity which is not humble. Rote conformity can and will come from a person who is set on doing something regardless of whether it is right or wrong simply because it is what they want to do or have been told to do. The prideful and arrogant will set their own rules and will not, in humility, submit and be obedient.

Obedience, in and of itself, implies a choice which is to be made. Obedience without the possibility of being rebellious is not obedience. The word loses all of its meaning unless one submits their will, voluntarily, to the will of the one they love and yields themselves in humility.

So, then, we cannot have obedience unless a person has had a choice to be disobedient. Obedience loses its value and definition if it is rote conformity.

The theological implications of this for the Five Point Calvinists are staggering. Either persons have a free will (and therefore a choice) or they don't. Of course, the Calvinists will say that a person can exercise a choice, but at the same time they say the choice is already predetermined. Now, if the choice is predetermined and if they say a person does exercise a choice then they are saying that the choice is just a perfunctory matter. It was a case of just going through the motions. I don't believe that anything God did or anything that He requires of us was done to "just go through the motions."

Of course, the Calvinists, who are expert at "reasoning" themselves out of any tight corner, will delight in taking my logic apart. But, I think it is more well founded than the convoluted theological model they have invented.

The point is: does a person have a choice in salvation or not? If it is all predetermined then the concept of obedience is rendered false.

Chapter 15

The North Star of Society

The church has always been the moral and spiritual "North Star" of society. It has always stood between society and moral rottenness and it has been striving to show people the right way to live life and please God. The world knows that if it can compromise the church and cause it to be just like the world, then, it follows that the voice of the church will be silenced or made to become insipid. Once compromised it can't say a word to society about its actions but it must deal with its own moral and spiritual shift. The church will be so busy trying to be accepted that it will cease to remember what it is commissioned to do.

Many people say that the church must be like the world in order to attract its people. Then, they say, they can witness to them. You lose the witness in being like the world. Some say that Jesus identified with the sinners in order to save them. That is a totally different thing. He did not go about creating an environment to please the sinners so that they would come hear him preach and then be saved. He lived His life among the people of society but He always maintained a difference between Himself and them. That's why they respected Him and looked to Him for answers and healing. What Jesus did is that He responded to sinners in their need. He did not become like them in order to save them.

Jesus didn't need to create a spectacle in order to attract a crowd. He was the "Spectacle" Himself. If we have the "Spectacle" among us and if we are faithful to preach the Gospel and witness of Him, then we don't need to become like the world in order to attract and win them. We have the "Church Builder" Himself attracting the lost and drawing them to Himself (John 6).

We have lost our collective sense of shame. When people lose their personal sense of shame then it isn't long before the nation as a whole feels shame for nothing. People have lost their sense of shame before God. They are more worried about what people think than they are about what God thinks. If they can hide something from people then they think they are home free with God as well. The reason for this is that they really don't think God is there and that, if He is, He doesn't care or won't do anything about their shameful actions. He will just overlook them.

When a nation has no sense of shame then it speaks of the fact that they have lost their sense of moral and spiritual direction. When low morals are accepted then shame is not felt. The higher the moral and spiritual standard, the more profound the sense of shame. Because there is no shame, then there is no remorsefulness for sin. We will be remorseful for sin only if we know God is watching with grieved disapproval and impending judgment.

The secular society knows that as long as the church is doing its job properly, they can't do as they would like to do without being called into question by the only thing that has the solution for sin: the Church. So, they have set about to keep the church from doing its job. They want to limit the church's influence because they know that it is the church which stands between them and a life of license. Remember, if the church takes on the attributes of the world, (the current drift) and lowers its standards (a current fact) in order to be attractive to the world, then it has lost its right to point them in the proper direction toward Christ. We will have lost our ability to be the North Star of Society. The possession of the truth does not depend upon whether one is relevant or not.

Whether one is relevant or not is dependent upon the possession of the truth.

We are, in our day, trying to be so relevant that we are giving up our unique ability to stand against the spiritual and moral decay of our day. We must return to a sense of sanity and focus on what is the primary purpose of our worship. We are not the focus, God is. We exist to glorify Him in our worship and in our work. What the church is largely doing today is employing the "Disney-like" methods of the world in an attempt to do God's work. These methods are worldly in their origination and God's work is founded and energized by heaven. If worldly methods are employed to try to accomplish a heavenly task it will never work but will only produce confusion and misdirection. And, that's where we are today in the majority of our churches. It is not our evaluation of success that matters. It is what God calls success that matters. He does not tell us to find any method to achieve what we consider success. He tells us to be faithful, deliver the Biblical message and let Him determine what happens.

Chapter 16

The Peace Prophecy Brings

During my thirty one year tenure as Pastor of the great Abilene Baptist Church, I preached three series of expository messages through the very interesting and compelling Book of Revelation. I found that our people always responded in a very powerful and positive way to the preaching of this great book. There was always a heightened sense of interest and energy among our people as they followed the study through Revelation.

The reason the subject matter of Revelation is always of interest is because we get a glimpse of what is to be and we are told in advance that *we win* in the cosmic battle between good and evil in the universe. Revelation, while it is a fascinating study of prophecy, it is also one of the most comforting books in the Bible.

As one studies the prophecies concerning the end of time which are contained in the Bible, they are able to see that many of the things which are happening today are part of the unfolding future of the world. God is not limited to a historical time line as we are. We are locked into history and He is in eternity and can see the full time line of things we will have to wait to experience. The prophets of old could give us prophecies which always come true because God allowed them to see points of history from His perspective. So what they saw is always going to take place because they were looking at events God has already placed in order. It is a good thing for us to pay attention to what the prophets such as John say to us concerning God's unfolding plan of history and redemption.

As we watch history unfold in our day to day lives we can take heart in the fact that nothing that happens catches God by surprise. And, there is nothing that happens which He does not give His People the ability to deal with. When I think about this, it gives me a peace and comfort in my soul where unrest might try to find a home. Why did God give us the prophets and their messages? It was to warn His People, both in the Biblical day and in our day, of things which were going to appear in history so that we could make sure that we were equipped to live through various situations. Of course, the world does not see the various present day world events in the light of Biblical prophecy. They can't understand what is really happening. We can get a glimpse of things as they really are and not just as they seem to be.

It would be wise of God's people if they would listen to the prophecies in His Word and consider them as a warning. It would also be wise if we would make provisions to deal with those warnings, if indeed, they came true in our day. We should make plans taking the prophecies into account so that God's warning to us would not be wasted. If we do then God can always say "I told you what was coming and you didn't listen or make provision for it. You will not have to suffer the consequences of your lack of vision and faith in My words."

This world situation we are in is not primarily political. It is not primarily economic in nature. It is not just a social upheaval. It is primarily a spiritual battle and we have a front row seat knowing all along how the game is going to end. That is a great advantage for God's people and one for which we must thank Him.

Chapter 17

The Sinister Nature of "Small" Sins

Man has fallen into a trap where sins are concerned. Not only does he commit them but he also has a way of "grading" them in order to give himself some leeway concerning judgment upon what he calls "small sins". Of course, murder, rape, sexual impurity and such are recognized as things which are always under the glare of God's judging eye. People will condemn each other for committing such acts and they think that God looks upon those things as especially horrible. God even mentions some of those things that the unsaved, worldly people will do. Fornication, lying, stealing, immoral living and adultery are just a few of the things that God says are particularly bad. So, because God points out a few that are particularly abhorrent to Him, we think that somehow the "lesser sins" are something that He really doesn't pay much attention to.

Wrong.

The thing that man fails to understand is that God is a *holy* God. We all agree that He is a good God but He is far more than that. He is a *holy* God and His holiness separates him from even one little microbe of sin. He will not tolerate one modicum of sin in His presence and that is not because He is just particular, but because holiness is His *nature*, not just a preference on His part. So, His holiness demands that there be no sin whatsoever in His presence. This is something that people just don't get. They think that since God is so interested in the "bigger sins" He will overlook or pay no attention to our "smaller" sins. Just remember: *All* sin is serious to God. He does not grade it at all and if left unredeemed, any sin will keep one from entering into God's presence.

God is so holy and separate that what we consider small sins are of major importance to Him. Satan was cast out of heaven not because he picked up a sword against God. He did not gather up his army and attack God. Those would have been major actions. No, he simply thought a thought which said, "I can do His job and sit in His place." "I'm going to be like God." Isaiah 14:12-17. When Satan thought such a thing, it offended God and Satan had to go. It was a major thing to God because it was rebellion against Him and rebellion against Him is a sin.

So, then how can we escape if small sins are not on a graded scale of importance or judgment? There is only one way. We must be prepared in such a way that God cannot see our sins large or small. In His sovereignty, God has decided that only one thing will keep Him from seeing our sins and that is the covering of the Blood of Christ. When we are covered, then God does not see those sins since he has decided that the Blood completely covers us and makes us acceptable in His presence. Without the Blood of Christ, our sins are staring God in the face because nothing else will satisfy Him and cover them. When our sins are covered with the blood then they are forgiven and because they are forgiven and covered they are forgotten.

Our "small" sins are particularly insipid. They don't bother us. We learn how to live with them thinking that since they are not one of the "major" sins we can simply dismiss them and God won't care. We rationalize them away in our minds but rationalization and repentance are not the same thing. We might get to the point that the "small" sins really don't bother us anymore and since they don't bother us then God must be overlooking them. That is why "small sins" have such a sinister nature about them. They must be redeemed just as the "bigger" sins must be. If a counselor convinces us that we have committed a sin because of certain events in our lives, that is not the same as repentance or forgiveness. Getting comfortable with our actions offers no protection. Small sins will sneak up on our blind side. "Everyone is doing it so I am not in the boat by myself", we will say. Remember whether you are in the boat by yourself or not is not the issue. Unredeemed sin is the issue and sinister "small" sins are particularly dangerous because we really don't understand the nature of God and His holiness.

God tells us to live holy lives. How can we do that? It is possible only if we will listen to the indwelling Holy Spirit of God who is given to us at the moment we are saved. If we listen intently to Him, He will guide us into all righteousness. God has never demanded something of His people that He did not given them the ability to do. If He did such a thing then He would be locking them into disobedience. So, He provided the Holy Spirit to guide us. We have no excuse because we have that provision which will guide us into a righteous, holy life. Sin, large or small, does not sneak up on a Christian. The Holy Spirit will tell us it is coming down the road even before it gets to us. When Christians sin, they have chosen to do so. It is their fault, but God has provided a covering and we find ourselves clean before him through the Blood of Jesus. That is His provision that allows us into His holy presence. What a wonderful, loving and forgiving God we have!

Chapter 18

The Straw That Broke the Camel's Back

When I was a young man of fourteen years of age, our family acquired its first television set. It was a black and white television and we had a tall antenna on top of our house with a motor to rotate it toward distant stations. In those days we only had two stations to view. One was an NBC station in Albany, Georgia and the other was in Tallahassee, Florida/Thomasville, Georgia. We mainly watched the Albany station because the reception from Tallahassee/Thomasville was not as good.

People in those days did not watch television all day. Children did not keep their eyes glued to a television screen. We still played outside in those days. But at certain times everyone would come into the house to watch programs. I remember *Disney's Wonderful World of Color* as well as the *Ed Sullivan Show*. No one ever missed those programs. There was another program which was always viewed with great interest. The NBC Nightly News with Chet Huntley and David Brinkley was our source of information in this wide, wide world. These two men were like members of the family. They were trusted and revered. The news they delivered was grounded in fact and not opinion. They brought us the story on events which were happening around the globe and we watched and listened with great interest and trust. On the CBS television network, Walter Cronkite was just as well liked and trusted. In fact, he was listed as the most trusted man in America at one point. Yes, there was a day in which network news was a good friend and it did not betray the trust and friendship of the American people.

A number of years ago things began to change. The network news became a source of opinion as much as it was a source of news. In the sixties there was a shift as the networks found out just how much power they had in their hands. Such trust had been built up in the fifties that no one wanted to question the men they had always allowed into their families at six o'clock each evening. This continued throughout the seventies and worsened in the eighties. The nineties saw no relief from the direction that the national news media had chosen for itself, and people were growing weary of always having to deal with a liberal leaning press. But something changed.

In the last decade of the twentieth century, the 1990's, there were a couple of developments. First, back in the early eighties CNN came into being and began to eat into the network news market. In the nineties, the internet and a proliferation of other news outlets joined in to deal network news a reeling blow. Their market share began to drop and it has continued to this day. Once everyone gained their news from the old network sources of ABC, CBS and NBC but now those outlets were struggling with falling viewer ship. FOX News came on the scene and only exacerbated the situation for the networks. But the main foe they are facing is the Internet. People are turning away from network news to their own personal news source on the internet. They can access it at any time in the privacy of their home and they can read and absorb as much as they like at any one moment. In addition a person can go to those sites which are known to be conservative or liberal. They don't have to sift through all the rhetoric in order to decide just what an author is trying to say. The internet has given individuals more control over the news they consume.

Never in the history of journalism has the public witnessed network news as biased in its coverage as during the 2004 Presidential

The Straw That Broke the Camel's Back

race for the White House. Many different sources have noted the fact that coverage has been unashamedly liberal in its approach. CBS has besmirched an already damaged reputation even further with their unending desire to break some sort of story which would be damaging to a sitting President. Dan Rather damaged his credibility beyond repair. Not only did one story disintegrate on him while he was still smacking his lips at the prospect of hurting the credibility of the President, but he and CBS never gave up. When the "documents" story imploded under the weight of its own false nature, they worked underhandedly with the *New York Times* to break another one about missing munitions. Dan Rather, not learning his lesson only a few weeks before, was going to break what he hoped would be a story which would swing the election toward the candidate he favored. This story blew up in their hands. CBS and Dan Rather were planning to break the story on Sunday evening just before the election but the *New York Times* broke it too early and when the facts got out they all stood there with smut all over their faces. This was a crucial error for CBS and it will have implications for network news beyond their own organization.

Additionally, NBC and ABC are just as biased and liberal as is CBS. They just have not been caught with two bogus stories. However they have participated in the greatest whitewash of a political candidate in years. The Democratic candidate got 77% favorable news stories from the major networks while the Republican candidate only managed to get favorable stories 34% of the time. That is too wide a spread to be accidental.

This writer believes that the network news media, including CNN, have sealed their fate. The way they have been so biased in their approach and coverage is The Straw that Broke the Camel's Back. I think that, in general, the people of the United States are going to be through with them.

They will no longer trust them and look to them for information as they once did. Not only are the American people tired of being manipulated by the media but they are also extremely fatigued at having their intelligence insulted. So, the downward turn of the national network media consisting mainly of the Big Three (NBC, CBS and ABC plus CNN) will continue. They will not disappear from the American scene but the massive hemorrhage of viewers and trust will not abate and is the natural by-product of their chosen direction over the last number of years.

They deserve it.

Chapter 19

The Translation Craze

Recently, while browsing in a Christian bookstore, I suddenly became fully aware of the number of translations of the Bible which are offered to the public today. Since the Bible is the most often read book in the world one would assume that it would require a number of translations or versions in order to satisfy the buying public. Certainly, it is not hard to see that the demand has been met. While many people might think that this is good in every aspect, I would like to direct the reader's attention to something which I think it would be to our advantage to consider.

As a Christian and a pastor of a local church, I understand the presence of different versions. In fact, I use several different translations when I am doing my research and study for a sermon. They are valuable sources for understanding what a particular passage is saying. I personally use the *King James Version in the New Scofield version* for my preaching and reading. I know Pastors who employ the *New International Version* and others who prefer the *Revised Standard Version*. The presence of different translations does not bother me because I understand that they are versions of original Greek manuscripts. However, as I was browsing that day I noticed something which, upon further reflection disturbs me. The list of versions and editions is growing at a quantum pace. Listed below are some of the offerings:

Bullseye: Perceptive Reflections on a Collapsing Culture

The King James Bible, the *New King James Edition*, *The Amplified Bible*, *Today's English Version (Good News for Modern Man)*, *The New Jerusalem Bible*, *The Living Bible*, the *New American Standard Version*, the *New Century Bible*, the *NIV*, the *Revised Standard Version*, the *New Revised Standard Version*, the *Revised English Bible* and the *New Living Bible*, were all for sale along with some others. In addition to those versions, there were a number of editions available. Those included: the *International Inductive Study Bible*, the *Cambridge Annotated*, the *Woman's Study Bible*, the *Spirit Filled Bible* (I didn't know there could be any other kind), the *Prophecy Study Bible*, the *Experiencing God Study Bible*, the *Life Application Bible*, the *Nelson Study Bible*, *Thompson's Chain Reference Bible*, the *Quest Study Bible*, the *NIV Rainbow Study Bible* and the *Dake's Annotated Reference Bible*.

There are many others not included in the list above, but as one can readily see, a person has no problem when it comes to finding a Bible to suit his needs. I think, however, that the unsaved people of the world are confused as are the less than dedicated people who claim Christianity. Let's make no mistake about it. Most of those issuing new Bible versions are driven by the profit motive, and I believe that the wrong message is being sent to those who are looking for answers to life's questions. Let me explain. People are told that the Bible is God's Word and that it is unchanging and stable. They can depend on it. It will guide their lives and lead them to salvation. But, the unsaved people of the world, and the carnal Christians look at all the versions and editions offered and they begin to see the Bible as nothing more than another book offered in different garb. Which one, they ask, should I believe? Which one has the right answers? Which one is the best one? Who is the best editor or publisher? I believe that the rush to profit in marketing the Bible is producing confusion, even among some Christians, about the utter truthfulness of the most trusted translations.

The mad rush to put yet another translation on the shelves is resulting in a product which is supposed to meet the "felt needs" of every little niche of society. People need to understand that the Bible meets *all* needs and does not have to be wrapped in a beautiful cover designed for a certain market segment in order to do so. God's Word should stand above all of these marketing schemes. In the eyes of many people it casts doubt on the seriousness of God's Word if it can be manipulated in such a way. It is hard to explain to a lost person that the Bible is the Bible, and if the translation is a reliable one, it does not matter about all the accompanying hype. I simply feel that people must be careful in how they handle God's Word. It is not given to us to market like some new line of clothes or some popular brand of automobile. And, if we allow this to happen, then people will pay less attention to what is on the inside and more attention to how it was marketed. This is a dangerous situation because someone with an inferior translation or one which serves a particular cult just might be very successful in getting their erroneous material into the hands of a lot of people who would, all along, be thinking that it was perfectly alright because it is "God's Word".

In addition, church people are confused about what to use. Many of them can hardly keep up with the Pastor as he reads scripture or preaches an expository sermon because so many of them have bought a Bible which is of a different translation. Scripture memorization is also suffering. No version can match the King James for it beautiful language. It lends itself so easily to memorization. For many years the KJV was the "Bible of the people" in the SBC, but that is now changing rapidly. At the same time fewer and fewer of our people can quote scripture. I am not a KJV only advocate but it sure is hard to beat when it comes to teaching your people the Bible.

We have gone translation crazy, and it now seems almost impossible to do anything about it because those driven by the profit motive will not stop since their primary concern is sales and not the Bible itself.

Since the rush to new translations and editions is not likely to stop, it must be left up to the Pastors to guide their people through the maze. Our people will trust us to give them the proper guidance and we must not fail to do so. It is up to us, by and large, not to fall into the current popular frame of mind concerning translations but to guide our people properly.

Chapter 20

Think About This

I think that it is high time for Christians in America to stand up and demand that our faith be treated with respect. Our country was founded upon the Judeo-Christian ethics in the Bible but this politically correct society wants to deny that fact and relegate Christianity and Christians to the trash heap of history. Generally speaking, the society in which we live is more than ready to do away with Christianity than we Christians would ever believe. An amoral, humanistic, liberal society has more respect for the other world religions than it does for the faith upon which our country was founded: Christianity. Some would argue with me about our being founded upon Christianity but I urge them to simply go and read our foundational documents and listen to the quotes from some of our founding fathers. There is no doubt about what their intentions were. It is clearly stated that America was founded to "propagate the Gospel of Jesus Christ" and that the Bible is absolutely necessary for the proper governance of people.

This brings me to the fact that we should not be reticent to let the people of the world know that we are a Christian nation and that they need to understand that when they come here. No one from any other religion should be surprised to hear a Christian prayer which ends with "in Jesus' Name, Amen." They should expect that. If I were in Arabia, I would expect to hear a Muslim cleric pray in their fashion and I would not be offended. I could pray silently in my own way. But, in America, we are expected to forget our Christian heritage and foundation and make room for everyone else to the point that we are not supposed to offer a decidedly Christian prayer. I think this is foolish and destructive to our American culture. It is most of all dishonoring to Jesus Christ.

I think a person should be able to worship as they see fit in America, but don't tell Christians that they have to change what they do simply because others have come here.

In Saudi Arabia a Christian is not allowed to worship or speak of his faith to others. They certainly can't pray a Christian prayer in public. That is true in other Muslim countries as well. But here, we allow them to worship in an unhindered way. In Indonesia many Christians are dying simply because they are Christians but here they worship as they desire. In India Christians are persecuted and killed in many areas of the country simply because they are Christians. In Somalia, thousands of Christians are dying because they won't convert to Islam. But, in the U.S. all people can worship as they choose with no fear of reprisal. Even further than that, we Christians are not supposed to have the same freedom because we might offend someone of another religion. This has got to stop!

There are many "special" programs which have been produced to denigrate Jesus Christ. The accounts of his birth, death, burial and resurrection have been brought under suspicion and critical analysis with the general conclusion being that the events of the Bible are simply not true. One should remember that any time a secular group deals with spiritual things, especially Jesus Christ, they will "goof it up" royally. They are incapable of understanding these things because they are seeking to deal with Godly spiritual principles with unredeemed minds. We have been told through the media that Jesus was married and had children. We have also been informed of the fact that they have found a bone box that contained the bones of Jesus. Jesus was not born in Bethlehem but in Nazareth. There was no special star announcing His birth but an alignment of planets which produced a bright light. He only "swooned" on the cross and the coolness of the tomb revived Him. And, oh yes, He is the illegitimate son of a Roman soldier. Jesus was married to Mary Magdalene and had children by her. He even sinned like we do. And, the list could go on and on.

Let me ask this question: Why don't they write books and make movies that say things like that about Mohammed? Just ask Salman Rushdie why they won't write such things or make such movies. They won't produce such things about Mohammed because they fear the results. They know the Muslims will not put up with it and that the consequences are severe, even deadly. But Hollywood and book publishers are not afraid of Christians because they know we don't react that way and we never will. We will handle them with grace and pray for them. We will endure the persecution while all the time trusting in God to deal with it properly. They know they won't get executed or persecuted if they slander Jesus. But, I want them to remember something: God is keeping the score and He is not going to let those who dishonor and slander His Son escape the consequences. Hollywood had better be careful because they are dealing with the Son of God and He is supreme in this universe.

Chapter 21

This Thing Called Transparency

At the outset of this commentary, it should be stated that the opinions stated herein are the by-product of closely watching the actions of people over the years. It would be human nature for one to read this article and try to attach names to it. If one does so then they are doing something this author is not intending.

So much is happening so quickly in the universe of our Southern Baptist Zion that people cannot absorb all that is being said and done. Many things are sliding right past the conscious minds of people which are extremely important. Fewer people are analyzing what is being said and more of them are evaluating things based on personal feelings and what "just seems right to me." A good example of what this writer sees is this thing we call transparency. Everyone wants to be known as a person who is honest, clean, wholesome and transparent. Transparency is nothing more than a public and personal display of a life which is based on truth and goodness. It is a characteristic of a life lived in such a way that the one living it doesn't mind if anyone and everyone sees him as he actually is. He is open. He welcomes investigation knowing that one will find nothing that he would not want discussed or openly known.

Transparency is not a trait a person acquires only after they are caught in some sin or failure. For one to suddenly desire transparency when he is caught is like the thief who is sorry for his actions only after he is arrested.

Suddenly the person seeks to appear noble by being transparent. Why wasn't he so interested in that transparency before? If he had been, then he probably wouldn't have found himself in a pickle because he was involved in some action that he could not be transparent about. But, all of a sudden, with his hand in the cookie jar, this person tries to engender some sense of nobility and honesty by showing people how sorry he is and how transparently he can deal with it.

There is a huge problem here that most are letting go right past them. Most people will extol the virtues of the transparency of the person involved. They will speak of him in glowing terms and point to his bravery and honesty. Remember, by this time the person is appealing to honesty and transparency only because it pays him to do so. The failing fades into the background as the quality of transparency is elevated to a status that it does not command. The problem is that many people will reveal their lack of spiritual maturity by equating transparency with repentance. Repentance deals with sin in the right way. Transparency does not deal with the sin. It only begs for tolerance in how the person is evaluated or treated. The Holy Spirit of God will lead us into a life that can be lived in a transparent way. The world and its sinful ways will cause a willing person to fall into that which must be hidden. So, just because a person is suddenly transparent, we must not ascribe to him some kind of noble status which is far short of repentance. This writer has noted that those who suddenly become transparent under pressure will reveal only what is necessary. One will often find that there is more to the story which the sudden transparency didn't get around to dealing with.

My concern is that we can observe that many people confuse transparency with repentance and are perfectly happy with their conclusion. The individual who is suddenly so transparent is held up as a spiritual person of high moral character due to his willingness to "come clean" and be transparent. One living in obedience to the guidance of the Holy Spirit will not find himself in such a position as having to appeal to transparency for survival and sympathy. Remember, a person begging transparency is usually doing so because he is caught and facing severe consequences.

So, the point is made. Transparency is not and cannot be equated with repentance. One would have to be evaluating a spiritual situation from an emotional position to think that it can be. In fact, for a person to have to appeal to transparency in the midst of a discovered sin is for them to use it for a selfish purpose when that very quality, transparency, should be a normal by-product of a godly life. To have to appeal to it says that it was not a part of that person's life beforehand.

May we all live our lives in such obedience to the guidance of God's Holy Spirit that we would live transparency and not have to appeal to it.

Chapter 22

Two Different Stories with Two Different Reactions

Author's note: While the people and events in this commentary time-date the piece, the main point is, nevertheless, well taken.

Much has been written over the last few years about the liberal bias that is exhibited by the media in this country. By "media" I am referring to movies, television and the printed media. Of course, as one would expect, the liberal media denies that they are liberal at all. They go to extremes to try to convince the public that the real problem is simply conservative paranoia. I want to examine this in the light of two current productions which flag the truth about just what the liberal establishment is trying to do using movies and television.

First there is the CBS miniseries about the Reagans. While Ronald Reagan is incapacitated with Alzheimer's disease and unable to defend himself, the liberal media is trying their best to do a hatchet job on one of the greatest Americans and Presidents we have ever had. He virtually, single handedly brought a conclusion to the Cold War. He was the main personality in the fall of communism. Ronald Reagan brought a sense of sanity and "rightness" to the White House which we desperately needed. He instituted an economic policy which brought a tremendous boom after the "malaise" of the Carter years. So, now Hollywood is trying to do a hatchet job on him and Mrs. Reagan by having them say and do things in the production which, even the author admitted, did not take place. He is depicted as a buffoon who bumbled his way through the presidency while being morally corrupt and foul mouthed at the same time. Mrs. Reagan is shown as the "boss" of the White House and government policy. She is also depicted as slapping her daughter and as a tyrant in general.

The question is, Why would anyone want to produce such a miniseries? The answer is simple. The liberal establishment wants to discredit anyone who was or is a conservative and who out-leads them and out-thinks them. The part of Ronald Reagan is played by none other than James Brolin the not-so-good-actor husband of ... you guessed it, Barbra Streisand. The situation is so obvious that it insults the intelligence of the American public. A big hue and cry has been made over this production to the point that CBS is now canceling it and taking a nine million dollar write off. It serves them right. Millions of people have contacted them threatening a boycott of the network and the sponsors of the program if it were to show. The program may be sold to Showtime which is so corrupt they don't care what they show, but at any rate it will not be on a national network, CBS in prime time.

The second program which was shown on ABC on Monday evening, November 3rd, was the program which "examined" whether Jesus was married to Mary Magdalene or not. This program was so poorly put together and so tainted by ultra-liberal ideas that it was a complete "hoot." It just goes to show one just how far liberals will go with their empty reasoning and suppositions in order to try to propagate their point of view. The premise was that Leonardo da Vinci secretly painted hints into his paintings concerning the fact that Jesus was married. So many holes can be shot in their weak, godless theory that there is not enough time or space here to do it. Nor would I want to spend my time answering such trash. Elizabeth Vargas, the host for the show said that the producers were going to handle the "information" as professionally as possible.

Two Different Stories with Two Different Reactions

My question again is: Why was the program necessary at all? Let me offer an answer to that question. I think that the politically correct society in which we live wants to discredit Jesus Christ as much as possible because of His claim, "I am the way, the truth and the life, no man cometh to the father but by me." Jesus places an exclusive claim on providing salvation to mankind and the politically correct simply cannot fathom the idea that all the other world religions miss the mark. The exclusive nature of Christianity flies in the face of this PC world and Satan knows that if he is to do Christianity harm he must attack our foundation which is Jesus Christ. They want to bring him down to the level of ordinary men, strip him of his Divinity and thereby cast Him as no more than a prophet which is what Mohammed claimed to be. Their goal is to put Christianity in the melting pot of world religions and make it just another way to get to heaven. I wonder why they don't do a "hatchet" job on Mohammed. I'll tell you why—they would be in fear for their lives if they did. They know the Muslims would not stand for it. And they also know that a price would be put on their heads quickly. Just ask Salman Rushdie who wrote a book which Muslims thought slandered the Koran. But, the politically correct liberals don't fear Christians because they know we are not a violent people with a violent religion. They know we are people of grace and love and that we would pray for them instead of placing a bounty on their heads. That's why you don't see them approaching Mohammed the way they are willing to approach the subject of Jesus.

The thing I want to point out about this is that while there was a hue and cry over the movie about Reagan, very little was said about the Prime Time production about Jesus. I think Christians need to look around and see what is happening to them. We don't need to be complacent just because America has always been Christian. It is time we stand up and demand the respect that Christianity deserves. This country would not be in existence and its government would not be such as it is without the Judeo-Christian ethics inculcated in our founding documents. Christians should make sure they "sound off" loud and clear when Hollywood or anyone else steps on Jesus Christ and Christianity in general. It is time to demand the respect that the PC world is so willing to give others.

Chapter 23

Virtues are Still Virtues

In the past few days it has been revealed that Dr. Bill Bennett, the author of the *Book of Virtues* as well as other notable works, has been spending time in the gambling casinos of Las Vegas and Atlantic City. It seems that, according to the casino's records, he has lost millions, but he says that he has broken about even. The amount of money he has lost or won is not the issue. The issue is that Bill Bennett, Drug Czar, former cabinet member for education, author and speaker whose main message has been virtue or the lack of it in society, has taken part in an activity which is far less than virtuous.

Liberals are giddy over the prospect of being able to roast a conservative like Bill Bennett. And, they are doing a good job of it at the present. However, the public needs to understand something. The liberals are trying to convince the public that not only is Bill Bennett a hypocrite, but that everything he has said about morality is wrong because of his actions. This author is not taking up for Bill Bennett and his gambling activity, but it is extremely important that the virtues which he has so ably written about should not be cast aside simply because Bill Bennett has disappointed everyone who ever looked to him for his word on the moral issues in America. And, that is exactly what the liberals want to do. They want to denigrate the moral positions Bennett has taken and say that those positions are open for debate simply because Bill Bennett has "fallen".

When one reasons this thing out, those who are attacking Bennett for gambling are themselves essentially saying that gambling is wrong; otherwise, where is their case? Bennett has stood for what is right and they are attacking him for gambling which betrays the fact that they think gambling is a vice and is therefore wrong. We should thank the liberals for affirming what we have always said about gambling; that it is wrong and harmful.

But, while we might be analyzing Bill Bennett and the damage this revelation has had to him personally, I think that we should also take a look at how society at large feels about it. There was a poll on the World Net Daily web site which brought alarm to me. This poll shows that we need to talk much longer and much louder about virtues than we have. Those who read the World Net Daily site are typically conservative people who generally express very conservative opinions in the various polls offered on the site. But this one concerning Bill Bennett and his gambling reveals something very disturbing. One would think that the majority of the people would have said that Bill Bennett was a hypocrite but that is not what happened. Only 11.95 percent said that he is a hypocrite. The biggest percentage, 29.41% said, "It's surprising, but no big deal". Nearly 16 percent said, "If you have the money, what's the harm?" "Good for him, there's nothing wrong with it" got 7.52 percent. My response was, "No big deal???" You would think it would be a huge deal to people who are even acquainted with who Bill Bennett is. I think this graphically displays for us once again just how far society has slipped. Now, here is the icon of virtuous thought being found out as a gambler and its "no big deal"? Something is terribly wrong here. I think it proves that people like to talk about the value of virtues and good morality but so many of the people don't let those virtues and values influence their lives.

Virtues Are Still Virtues

Additionally, it must be pointed out that the failure of the man does not negate what he has said. Virtues do not slide up and down a scale which is set to the actions of Bill Bennett or anyone else. They are not right or wrong based on whether the person who stated them is right or wrong. Moral virtues are right. God stated the basics of them long ago in the Ten Commandments and other Biblical passages. Bill Bennett is a good man who has stated many good things which would make our nation better if they were followed. But he is a good man who made a bad mistake. God can forgive him for that, but the sad thing is that people will not. They will never forget it, and the liberals will never tire of trying to take the failings of Bill Bennett and turn them into an argument against the good things he has stated concerning good virtues and Godly morality. And, that is the real tragedy is this whole thing.

Chapter 24

We Are Right and You Must Agree

For those involved in the work of the Southern Baptist Convention (SBC), the effort to bring the SBC back to the theological position of some, but not all, of its founders has taken on a growing new life among us.

What I am going to say about this will undoubtedly be misunderstood by some. Others will ignore what I say. There are some who just aren't into the whole thing. Still others, especially those who are sympathetic to the movement, will simply try to find something for which to respond in a negative way.

Let me "steal a little of their thunder" at this point. While I am a pastor and Bible student of the last thirty-seven years, I get the feeling at times some of my Calvinist brothers perceive me as simply "ignorant and uneducated" and therefore, "can't grasp" the positions of those who hold Five-Point Calvinism as their theological model. Apparently I am "unread", having never read any of the cited confessions and certainly too "dim witted" to grasp anything that Spurgeon, Whitefield and others have espoused concerning Calvinism.

Like it or not, that is the kind of thing that is thrust upon someone like me. Indeed I also get the feeling that, once Calvinism is properly explained to me by my Calvinist brothers, they fully expect me to switch my theological positions and join the ranks of the Five-Point Calvinist group!

I'm reminded of the Charismatics in the mid 70's who implicitly stated that "when you have *our* experience then you will be as spiritual as we are and you will have arrived." Didn't work then. It isn't about to now.

Recently I was talking with a very dedicated Christian man who is a Calvinist although not a five-pointer of the more modern day radical variety. We have been very good friends for a long time and the Calvinism thing has never been a problem for either of us.

Why was it not a problem given the hyper state of the discussion in the SBC these days? The reason it is not a problem for my friend and me is twofold. First, we *both* accept the fact that the other is saved. In the course of a good, friendly but lively exchange, I asked him a question that is very pertinent, "Do you think I am saved?" He answered, "Absolutely." Then I said, "Well, I think you are saved also." What follows is simple common sense. If he thinks I (a non-Calvinist) am saved, and I think that he (a Calvinist) is saved then *salvation is not the issue. Instead, the core issue is one's theological model and methodology.*

Secondly, we both agree that it takes *repentance and faith in Christ in order to be saved.* That is the bottom line of our fellowship; not whether I adopt his theological model or not.

So, just how does this apply to the conflict over Calvinism in the SBC? *As I see it, the issue that is troubling the SBC is the insistence that a person and ultimately the convention agree with the Calvinist position concerning the process of salvation.* In other words, *we are right and you must agree.* That is, one must conform to their position.

My question is, "If I said to these individuals, Okay, I accept your Five-Point Calvinistic model," would the disagreement and animosities cease to exist? Does one mean to tell me that if I would simply start agreeing with the Calvinists and adopt their theological position that all would be well? If I would agree with them then all the sniping and blasting directed toward those poor "misinformed" non-Calvinists would suddenly disappear?

Are the Five-Pointers actually willing to put the Convention through all the rhetoric and vitriolic verbiage just to hear people say that they capitulate and adopt their approach? If that took place would everyone be happy and would all the plotting to take the Convention back to the theological position of some of the founders of this great body of believers cease when, in reality, the vast majority of the people of the SBC do not hold to that particular theological model and, as an overall group, have not held it for a long, long time.

My difference of opinion with the Five-Point Calvinists is not founded upon the fact that they hold their position. I too, hold many of the same beliefs as they do. My disagreement with them is centered on the way that many of them go after churches in order to get them into the Calvinist camp.

A couple of years ago, I was taken to task in the blogosphere for simply pointing out that a Calvinist should not accept the call of a non-Calvinist church, failing to inform the people of his leanings and slowly but surely prod them in a surreptitious way toward his Five-Point position in an effort to get them to adopt his theological model. What happens in a host of cases—actually most of the ones about which I am aware—is that the church does not want to go there. Inevitably, a church fight erupts which splits the church, divides families and causes general confusion.

Conversely, I do not think a non-Calvinist should accept the call to a Calvinistic church and surreptitiously attempt to change it either. I was simply calling for the same thing that several of our noted convention leaders and others had called for—*integrity in dealing with a church that is trying to call a person to lead them.* And integrity demands we give the church the privilege of calling a person who agrees with them doctrinally without having to go through all the theological gymnastics in order to make sure of the theological position of their pastoral candidate.

More and more churches are finding that they have to be very specific in the questions they ask in order to get at the truth of a person's position because many of our Calvinist brothers know the Five-Point position won't fly in the majority of the churches in the SBC and they become very adept at talking around the issue while making the pulpit committee feel comfortable with them. This should not be done by Calvinists or non-Calvinists.

I might also point out that the non-Five Pointers such as myself and the vast majority of the people of our convention, did not create the current issue in the SBC which is becoming very divisive. It was created by the aggressive Five-Point Calvinists who insist that people agree with them and who are willing to push the issue to a breaking point just to hear people say that they will adopt their stance. I would hasten to add that not all Calvinists are part of those who hold such a position.

One of the major problems is that Calvinism has been taught more and more in the last few years. Consequently, many of the younger people ascribing to it have taken that theological position beyond the Calvinism of Spurgeon and the like. They have adopted an aggressive attitude which becomes very indignant and aggravated when people don't join them in their theological stance or when a person voices one word of caution or difference of opinion.

They display their immaturity in the way they use such hostile and vitriolic language as they attack people they really don't know. The hostility is palpable and it is, in most cases, a by-product of being young and having blood which is full of "spit and vinegar." Non-Calvinists have never really cared if a person was a Calvinist or not as long as they both believed and preached the Bible, and as long as they both tried to win the lost, and as long as advocates of neither viewpoint made a point of insisting that their theological position be adopted.

We Are Right and You Must Agree

Question: *Is agreement on Calvinism really worth all the vitriol and division that this unnecessary family argument is bringing?* What is going to be accomplished if Calvinists succeed? Would they then say, "Well, we are *all* saved, and we are *all* winning the lost of the world, but better still we won the *theological* argument"? Furthermore, "Everything we went through was worth it so that we could all hold the position that we, the Calvinists agree with." I think that we are paying too high a price for that and my fear is that it will get worse before it gets better.

Over the last couple of years I have been casually compiling a list of churches which have been bothered, disrupted and split by this issue. This list continues to grow as I become aware of such churches through conversations with others. The stories are all basically the same and they are tragic. Please hear me, *It is not tragic that a pastor holds a Calvinistic position.* Rather, it is tragic what happens to a church body when a pastor uses the above mentioned process to try to change a church's theological orientation from non-Calvinist to Calvinist and the people needlessly and unnecessarily suffer great trauma.

While at the SBC meeting in Louisville a couple of years ago, I received an e-mail from a person in South Carolina who has been communicating with me concerning Calvinism infiltrating their beloved church. She and her husband left a church where the pastor failed to inform the people of his positions and when those positions became apparent, the church went through some very difficult times. Sadly, this is the case with many churches.

As I stated at the beginning of this commentary, I know that, if past reactions to any criticism of the Calvinist position are the norm, I will be duly roasted, skewed and taken to task by people who don't even know me and furthermore couldn't care less if they did. I would simply say this in response to that possibility and probability, *I am doing nothing more than voicing what many, many people in the SBC are saying and thinking.* For one reason or another they simply don't want to get involved any further than giving their private opinion to another in a private setting. I can appreciate that but, quite frankly, I really don't care what someone might say about me. At this stage of the game I am not building a 'resume' and it really doesn't matter to me what anyone says. And, you know ... that's really liberating!

Chapter 25

What it Was, Was a Toothpick

It has often been said and most certainly verified by experience that the Federal Government can and most often does totally confuse and complicate everything it touches. In my mind's eye I can envision what would happen if the government were to assume the manufacture and distribution of one of the most essential of all human implements, the common toothpick. Now, we are all very familiar with this most necessary tool. With it we are able to remove unwanted food particles which are wedged between our teeth and seated around our gums. It has been in common use for hundreds of years and is found on most every table or in every cupboard of every kitchen in the country.

Somehow, it seems that all of a sudden some little pantywaisted bureaucrat who has never done anything of value in his whole life, decided that the populace would be much better off and indeed would find it essential if the Federal Government assumed the responsibility of manufacturing and distributing that little wooden sliver known as a toothpick.

As we let our minds wander down the paths that the bureaucrat's mind would naturally find attractive, we might ask ourselves this question, What would a toothpick look like and how would it operate if a Federal Government bureaucrat designed it? I propose the following.

First, each one would be pointed on only one end. The purpose of this design would be to keep people from sticking the other sharp end into their finger or under their fingernail thereby avoiding a trip to the doctor or emergency room. Every human being needs this kind of protection. Just think of the infections and pain which will be avoided.

Secondly, each toothpick would need a device designed to keep it from being swallowed or inhaled by someone who is a novice at picking their teeth. I can envision that the little anti-swallowing device would need to be big enough not to be ingested if some unforeseen and unfortunate occurrence took place such as a hiccup or a sneeze while in the act of extracting food from between the teeth. It would have to be mounted on the dull end of the toothpick and would need to be something that resembled a small umbrella in the opened position. Certainly this would be sufficient to protect the unwary or careless picker. The little umbrella would allow the sharp end of the toothpick to enter the mouth and do its job while the little umbrella would not go past the lips thereby keeping the person safe from choking while removing unwanted food stuck amongst their teeth.

Certainly, mused the little panty-waisted metro-sexual bureaucrat this would be a most brilliant and well accepted idea. It might take some getting used to but in the coming years people will praise the wisdom of the person who framed the design—or so he thinks.

Thirdly, each of these little federally designed utensils would have to have a serial number emblazoned on it to make sure that investigators would know where it was bought and where it was manufactured in case someone, somewhere was able to swallow the umbrella and succeeded in ingesting the toothpick which is now more akin to a device. In addition they would be able to find out who purchased the box of toothpicks and where they purchased it.

This will be most helpful when the study is done to ascertain the effectiveness of the design and also to help other panty-waisted bureaucrats to redesign the implement and present the populace with the improved model when the Toothpick Awareness PAC holds its meeting. These serial numbers will have to be printed with non-toxic ink and should be positioned on the side of the shaft near the little anti-swallowing umbrella device.

Fourthly, one would have to sign a form which attested to the fact that they had read the 227 page instruction manual just to make sure they know how to use the toothpick properly. Reading the manual entitled, The Proper Use of the Common Toothpick, will be absolutely necessary before a box of toothpicks can be purchased. Any grocery store, or other retailer who sold toothpicks to a customer without validating that they had read the instruction manual and that the purchaser was at least 18 years old, would be fined no less than ten thousand dollars and would be required to resign their job and do six months of public service to atone for their careless oversight and for breaking the federal law which applies to such cases. That law being unanimously passed by both houses of Congress and is entitled: The Federal Oral Food Particle Extraction Law. As one Congressman so nobly stated, "This law is one of the most important pieces of legislation that this august body has passed in the past 25 years. It will save hundreds of lives and will relieve untold human suffering. I am most proud of the fact that I have affixed my name to it." Upon completing the reading of the instruction book, The Proper Use of the Common Toothpick, the citizen will be presented a document suitable for framing which will attest to the fact that they have completely read the document and are therefore qualified to operate a toothpick in a safe manner.

Fifthly, the Federal Oral Food Particle Extraction Law stipulates that anyone who tampers with a toothpick will face prosecution to the fullest extent of the law. Such law mandates that anyone guilty of tampering will be forbidden from ever using a toothpick again in their entire life. They will be forced to live with food stuck between their teeth no matter how uncomfortable and unsightly it might be. Additionally, they will be shunned by people who are repulsed by the smell of their breath and the sight of the gum disease resulting from never again being able to use the new federally mandated toothpick. Those who tamper with the new toothpick rightly deserve such punishment.

Sixthly, each person who purchases a container of toothpicks must purchase a Federal Permit to operate the devices under the Federal Oral Food Particle Extraction Law. Such permit may be purchased on line or at the local Department of Social Services and may be obtained for the price of $371 annually. All eating establishments must purchase a toothpick permit for the number of patrons their establishment is designed to accommodate for any given meal. Any restaurant not displaying the toothpick permit will be forced to close by the end of the day in which their non-compliance is discovered.

In the coming decades people gathered around the dinner table will look at the new federally mandated toothpick and they will say, "Do you remember in the olden days when we had a little rounded sliver of wood sharp on both ends with which to pick our teeth?" Some little child at the table will chime in and say, "What did you use in the olden days daddy? What did you call it? To which the oldest member of the clan will reply, "What it was, was a toothpick." "And, my little dear, aren't you glad that our government cares so much for you that they want to make sure that you do not die or get injured by such a dangerous thing as we used to employ to clean our teeth?"

Section Two:
Quick Quotes and Pithy Sayings
by William F. Harrell

Quick Quotes and Pithy Sayings by William F. Harrell

Most of the quotes and sayings which follow are from my own musings but since nothing under the sun is new others have framed some of the same thoughts but used different words to express those thoughts. I know of none of the following entries which were taken from someone else's intellectual materials even though they may sound similar in some cases.

Many of the following sayings, quotes and thoughts are theological in nature while others are of a practical or secular nature. Some other entries are political and others are meant to be humorous.

WFH

- Jesus did not die on the cross with the idea that following Him was an option. His work was finished and complete. It provided the capacity and reason for us to follow Him.

- If one turned the intelligence of most Americans of today into gunpowder, it would not be enough to blow a gnat's brains out.

- Because worship (church) is no longer primary in society we have ceased trying to figure out how other things will affect it.

- When God says "Thou shalt not" He is on your side trying to save you a lot of trouble.

- Many people practice a "spiritual alternate lifestyle". It is called apostasy.

- Man is the only thing God created which can be and must be saved.

- The sacrificial death of Jesus provides the basis for man's capacity to be won.

- I have never had anyone say, "Alcohol has really been a wonderful blessing in my life."

- People see church attendance as an option—a good option but an option nevertheless.

- A proof that the Bible is the Word of God: If it were not God's Word, the world would believe it, but since it is God's Word, the world rejects it.

- All of the paradoxes of Scripture seem to be such only from our viewpoint. It is all very clear to God. A paradox is that point which is reached in reasoning beyond which the human mind is not capable of venturing but which is very clear to God.

- No one was ever saved or lost without God knowing about it.

- God has a spiritual process for getting you "in" Christ. Now, what is the process for getting you out? The obvious answer is that there is none. Once you are "in" you are eternally secure.

Quick Quotes and Pithy Sayings by William F. Harrell

- "When events come that we don't understand, we must remember that God has it all in hand."

- There is nowhere in the Word of God that God makes provision for a defeated Christian.

- If the inferior will let the Superior in him take over then the world will think that the inferior is superior.

- None of the world religions say one thing about being born again, and Jesus said that being born again is essential to salvation.

- We are the last generation to realize that the world has gone crazy. The present generation thinks things are normal!

- We are the last generation that has to wonder about anything. The answer to any question is at our fingertips through technology.

- Consistency keeps the devil from getting his foot in the door.

- We have created an environment in which the human heart feels comfortable in being desperately wicked.

- People are so consumed with their freedoms that they have put themselves in bondage.

- No constraints make for an environment in which the desperately wicked heart flourishes in its wickedness.

- We should so identify our Christian faith with the way we live as a country that the rest of the world would expect to find Christian things happening here and not be surprised or offended.

- Grace is receiving something you don't deserve. Mercy is not receiving something you do deserve. This is, of course, not original with me, but so true and meaningful that I included it here.

- From the most powerful to the weakest, we all have the same power and privilege in prayer.

- Without understanding the element of Grace, man will always think that he was somehow responsible for his own salvation.

- People have grown so sinful that they no longer care if God is offended, just so that they are not offended.

- The church of today has traded holiness for human ingenuity and worldly methods.

- God is a *good* God but He is more than that. He is the *holy* God which means that He cannot, by His nature, allow even one microbe of sin in His presence. Being holy is far, far beyond simply being good.

- Doing right and good things is not holiness. Holiness is not something you do but something you are.

- Humility is that quality that ceases to exist the moment one becomes aware of it. Don't ever tell a Godly, humble person that they are because at that moment they will cease to be.

- Holiness in a necessity, not an option. It can be achieved only when one realizes the necessity for it.

- We are living in strange times when immorality is glorified, excused and exalted; the physical trumps the spiritual and spirituality is exalted over salvation.

- A true Christian will feel the impulse to be separated from a sinful act.

- A person must come to Christ to flee God's wrath. Any other motivation misses the point of the coming of Christ.

- Life is not worth living if I can't live it in harmony with God through Jesus Christ.

- To preach a pure Gospel the Church must be pure and remain so.

- A Godly Christian life was never presented as an option.

- In tithing, a person demonstrates that they believe Jesus is Lord of *all* of life.

- Many people now believe that, "If you'll repent to some extent, you will be saved to some degree."

- When someone says, "The times have changed", we must remember that we are not tied to the times but to the Bible.

- There has never been a generation with as many reasons to believe that Jesus will return in their lifetime we have.

- Men throw broken things away. God never uses anything until He breaks it.

- People love the trip to hell but they just don't want to pay the price.

- Answered prayer is when the resources of heaven are supplied down here because we asked for them.

- The only "seats" in heaven are front row seats. Baptists need to understand that.

- When worship is brought down to the lowest common denominator of acceptability then we have made it a common thing.

- If one takes "holy" off the Bible and holiness out of the church, brings God down a notch or two, then the world doesn't look quite so bad.

- When the world rushes to a particular popular preacher and his methods then true Christians should be wise enough to take note of it and flee. If the world loves you and throws accolades on you then you have become common enough for them.

- Our worship must, to some degree, reflect and mirror the gravity of what took place on the cross because we could not be worshipping at all without what happened there.

- The Gospel and the cross are not marketable items. Their meaning for a person's soul is destroyed the moment it is taken and used in the way many are doing today because redemption depends ultimately on something other worldly. The other worldly element cannot be replaced with what we can produce.

- If *we* will be faithful in what we can do, then He will use us in building the church.

- To find out the will of God in your life, start somewhere serving Him and let Him take you to where He wants you to be. That place is the will of God for your life.

- God never promotes unfaithfulness.

- The actions and attitudes of people prove that they do not really believe that God is sovereign and all powerful.

- Too many preachers make people feel good in church and then send them out into the world lost but confident that because they feel good they are heaven bound. Wrong.

- The contemporary movement has made the preacher just another one of the boys. It has stripped worship of its aura and grandeur and made it just another activity that people can attend.

- In today's society the people have a lot of beliefs and opinions but few convictions. Opinions can change but convictions are something one will die for.

- The things which offer structure and discipline in society are being eliminated or re-defined so that the only "structure" is the lack of it.

- Being part of the Body of Christ and being part of a crowd are two different things.

- Man can produce a crowd, but only Jesus can build the church.

- Where sin is concerned, we are like a cold natured creature. Remember the frog in the kettle. Sin sneaks up on a person and they get used to it in degrees.

- Transparency concerning sin is not the same thing as repentance. In today's religious environment, repentance is being re-defined as transparency.

- People generally will be transparent about their sin as soon as they are caught.

- To pass along one's genetic makeup makes them a father. To pass along one's heart makes them a Dad.

- When principles are violated then problems are the result.

- Jesus never had to obey anything until the incarnation. He was the one to be obeyed. But after the incarnation, Jesus was subject to obedience.

- A person's morality overrides their education.

- The more Christ is "formed" in you, the less sin will be in your life and the more God will pay attention to you.

- God will not bless disobedience. If He did, He would have to violate His own nature of holiness.

- Peace with God is not the absence of problems. His peace is realized more when there is trouble and suffering in the life.

- When one is saved, they enter a war already won but must be willing to fight the battles.

- The only thing about a Christian that is not saved is the body but it too will be redeemed and transformed at the Resurrection.

- How one lives and not what they possess is what counts.

- Wicked people have fear as their constant partner.

- Trying to get rich quick will not pay off.

- A driving, freezing rain will not keep fans from a ball game, but a heavy fog will cause God's people to stay home and abandon worship.

- Any theology you preach must be applicable all over the whole world. If it is not, then it is invalid and erroneous.

- It is good to be able to laugh at yourself. It speaks of a healthy self-image.

- Poetic justice: When you act one way and later someone comes along and acts toward you in the same way.

- When God's Spirit and the human spirit work together, they will produce a holy life.

- The world can and does set some moral parameters on behavior. Living within the world's moral parameters is not the same as being saved.

- Jesus did so many astounding and transforming things that even walking on the water is given small billing in the Gospel accounts.

- Salvation did not originate on earth. It is a heavenly thing. When one commits their life to Jesus then God takes of the heavenly and applies it to someone in the earthly realm.

- Everything *man* does to be saved is of the earth and there is no saving power in it. It originated in the wrong place.

- The unsaved person is incapable of properly guiding themselves morally.

- Man is so selfish and self-centered that he thinks every desire he has is a *right*.

- If you wed the gravity of the cross with the levity of the world then you do the cross great damage.

- Our relationship to God is not on a "dues-paying" basis.

- Our worship should always, to some degree, mirror the gravity of what took place on the cross. Jesus did not say, "It is finished, now go and have yourselves a good time and actualize yourself."

- God does not forgive sin by overlooking it because the Blood of Jesus is invested.

- Man's dilemma is not that he needs more recreation, entertainment or convenience. Therefore, the church should not focus primarily on those areas as many do today.

- For God to bless America today, He would have to violate His own nature because He cannot bless disobedience.

- If the Gay Pride parade in San Francisco were to be shown on television nationwide, the homosexual movement would be dead in the water.

- A man may be lazy to the bone and not want to work all the days of his life but Satan can convince that same man that he must work like a slave all his life and do everything perfectly in order to get to heaven.

- When they crucified Peter upside down, they crucified a man who had *actually* walked on water.

- People refer to "safe sex." Sex is not supposed to be dangerous.

- God has commissioned me to tell you that you will go to hell if you live in your sins and reject His salvation through Jesus.

- Christ's death on the cross was meaningless unless there is eternal life. What's the point of His dying if, at some point, we cease to exist anyway?

- At the cross, man was at his worst and God was performing His best—the redemption of man.

- Samson was *handpicked* by God but *hen pecked* by Delilah.

- People have the right to believe anything they desire, but that does not mean that anything they want to believe is right.

- Being happy depends more on the spiritual than the physical.

- No one was ever mentioned in Scripture who was saved *twice*. It only happens once.

- If a person could "get saved" again, then they did not have eternal life the first time.

- God does not grade on a curve. In fact, He does not grade at all.

- There is no sliding scale of morality. What's moral is moral and what's immoral is immoral. This also applies to holiness and righteousness.

- Faith laughs at impossibilities and obedience raises no questions.

- Christianity is just another world religion to most of the people of the world. It is up to us to show them the relevancy of saving faith which comes only through Jesus Christ.

- If you are living like hell what makes you think you are going to heaven?

- Satan will convince a Christian that if they can remember their sins then they are still guilty and not saved. He makes a person feel guilty for something God covered with the Blood of Jesus and forgot.

- Physical death is not the most profound death—spiritual death is. The problem for man is that he does not have to die to be spiritually dead because he already is. We come here spiritually dead. In the physical realm one has to be alive before they can die, but in the spiritual realm life comes after death. God does things totally opposite from the way they happen on earth in the physical realm.

- Tithing is something we can do from an earthly perspective to bring God's blessings upon us. God does not need our money but He uses our obedience at the point of tithing to bring His blessings upon us.

- When we tithe and give an offering, *we* are determining how much God can bless us.

- A person of integrity remains constant no matter who is watching. He does the same thing in the closet he would do before men.

- God never instructs us to do something that He does not give us the power to do or else He would be locking us into a position of disobedience.

- Would you feel at home in heaven?

- In modern day Christianity, I am afraid we are trying to bring Christ down to our level instead of seeking to rise to His.

- What you don't arrive with, you can't leave with except one thing: Eternal Life.

- Satan has confronted "unfallen" man twice. First in the Garden of Eden and secondly on the Mount of Temptation. Jesus did not fall as did Adam and thereby became the basis of our Salvation. The righteousness of Christ imparted to a fallen man by faith, puts the fallen man in the spiritual position of the Unfallen Man—Jesus Christ.

- When a person compares his life to drunks, harlots and moral degenerates, he looks very good, but that is not the proper standard. When a person measures himself alongside Jesus Christ, the disparity is glaringly evident.

- The drawing away to sin by the OSN (old sin nature) is so strong that the only thing which can draw one the other way is God's Holy Spirit drawing men to Christ. Man can't do it; only God can.

- Satan attaches himself to the flesh; God attaches Himself to the spirit.

- One can only know what salvation is or is like after their sins have been remitted. One can have knowledge only of that which has happened. When sins are remitted, then salvation can be realized.

- Sinners love the trip to hell. They just don't want to pay the price.

- [The world says] The worst thing one can do to someone else in today's world is to tell them they are wrong and thereby hurt their feelings.

- Repentance is a word that is not heard much in today's church. [The world says] To tell one they need to repent implies they are a sinner and that implies they need to be saved which implies they are lost. It will insult people in our compromising society and if they are insulted then you are at fault and should apologize.

- Fighting the "good fight" Paul refers to does not mean that one always wins. The "good fight" is determined by ones faithfulness to the task, not the outcome.

- You are not giving to God if all you do is tithe. You can't give something that does not belong to you. You are not giving until you first tithe.

- Death is not just the separation of the soul from the body. Death is the separation of the Spirit from God.

- The value of salvation cannot be recognized unless there is an awareness of God's wrath.

- Christianity is not just something that it's nice to be a part of.

- Jesus did not come so that He could "fit into" your life. He came to give you new life.

- Truth is a foundation of Heaven and that's why the world prefers a lie.

- Christians should not be surprised when the world acts like the world is supposed to act, but we should be surprised when Christians act like the world. We have been empowered not to act that way.

- We should live like a resurrected Lord lives inside of us.

- The plan of salvation has never changed which points to the fact that human nature has not changed because the plan of salvation would have to be changed if human nature had been altered.

- Satan is not stronger than God and he doesn't have to be to win the battle in your life. He just has to be stronger than you. Then he can conquer you and get you to subvert God's desire for your life.

- In society, we are free only to the extent that we do not offend some judge's sensibilities or opinions.

- God cannot change for the better for He would not have been God in the first place. Neither can God change for the worse for then He would cease to be God.

- The world *abandons truth* for the sake of self; Christians *abandon self* for the sake of the truth.

- God is not in heaven saying, "Let's make a deal." He is in heaven saying "This is the deal."

- The first amendment does not say that you have freedom of speech except when you offend someone. It assumes that your freedom of expression just might offend someone.

- I had rather be morally right than economically strong. It would be nice if we could have both, but history has already proven that money corrupts the souls of men and therefore the soul of a nation.

- People want just enough of our medicine (Christianity) to make them feel better, but not enough to make them well.

- When the smallest things in life start becoming major issues to you then you are reaching overload and are in need of some relief.

- Being clean is more than just not having dirt on you.

- Most Christians are content to live beneath their spiritual privilege.

- We are what we are and we shouldn't make ourselves into whatever in order to please whoever.

- America's pulpits should be free to give guidance on issues that deal with morality and spirituality even if such guidance has to be political in nature.

- To the world, the church is the only barometer of whether Christianity is real or not.

- Most people really don't think that God has much influence in the lives of people or the events on planet earth.

- We will never see ourselves as we are until we see God as He is—Holy—"… high and lifted up."

- A person sees no need for a change until they have had an experience with God.

- People will lead careless, sinful lives as long as they think God really has little influence.

- To displease God is inconsequential to people until they are confronted with His Holiness.

- A visible sign that God has reconciled us to Himself is that we don't live under His wrath.

- Just because God *can* do something does not mean that he *has* to do it.

- One great trouble for modern man is that he does not want to bow down and worship anyone—not even God. Modern man is too proud, educated and erudite to subject himself to anyone.

- I am afraid that Christians don't witness because they don't enjoy what they have. They place no real value on their own Christian experience. If we really like what we are; enjoy what we are and value what we are, we will want others to experience it.

- One of God's greatest gifts to us is inward assurance. It cannot be reasoned into existence. It cannot be gained by any method. It is not for sale. It is granted; given by the only one who possesses it; God.

- Feeling you have eternal life and knowing it are two different things. Feeling is based on externals while knowing is based on the promise of God.

- God never has to wait on anything because He resides in the eternal *now*. We, being creatures of time and space, have to work our way forward on the time line of history to finally get to where God always was.

☖ Our society has reached such an ungodly point that people proudly display in the public forum those things they used to only whisper about in the most private of settings.

☖ The collective intelligence of Congress qualifies it for admittance to a mental institution.

☖ The Supreme Court does not hold session in Heaven.

☖ Everyone wants to be saved but most people don't think they need to change much.

☖ Salvation must, by its very nature cause a change. It must birth internal revolution against what a person once was.

☖ A television commercial for a lawyer said, "The secret for a successful bankruptcy is advanced planning." Now … there's a secret for success if I ever heard one!

☖ False prophets are really helping people commit eternal spiritual suicide. They are guilty of spiritual assisted suicide.

☖ You can't talk yourself out of something you have behaved yourself into.

☖ Do we think that God will excuse us from the guilt of murdering an unborn child simply because we tell Him that it is acceptable under our laws?

☖ The moral culpability of the producers of commercial alcoholic beverages is not diminished by the fact that they tell the public to "drink responsibly"

☖ All the bad choices of life are redeemed by one good one: Choosing *for* Christ.

- It is the church and the Bible which are preserving some sense of sanity in society. We are the only ones who have the desire or the authority or the power inherent in God's Word to do this battle and we must stand up to it.

- The church is the only invincible institution on the face of the earth. Everything else rises and falls but the Church has the promise that even the "gates of hell" shall not prevail against Her.

- "Spanktification" brings on sanctification!

- Today's church needs to be detoxified. It is intoxicated with its own desires, entertainment and liberal theology. It is drunk on itself as it seeks to reach God through secular means. It is inebriated with its pursuit of self-fulfillment with a semblance of spirituality.

- The "stuff" of our lives will gain our attention, determine our attitude and decide our actions.

- Ability is what you are capable of doing; motivation determines what you do and attitude determines how well you do it.

- With the current marketing strategies being applied to the church, man is growing an organization but he can never build the church because man is not the one who decides whether one is saved or not; the Lord does that.

- Being *saved* not just being *satisfied* is the issue.

- A man is better known by who his enemies are. One's friends will overlook many things because they are your friend. Enemies will overlook nothing in an effort to harm you or your reputation.

Quick Quotes and Pithy Sayings by William F. Harrell

- The fact that we are no longer recognized as a distinctive Christian nation is subtly revealed in the fact that the Gideon Bible is not the only religious material available in hotel rooms.

- Conviction and contrition are not the same thing. Conviction reveals sinfulness; contrition reveals sorrow.

- The church is *not* a charity. Tithing is *not* giving to a charity. It is giving to God that which already belongs to Him.

- The closer one is to God the more sensitive they are to sin.

- Always be careful of spirituality dressed in a slick outfit and espousing some esoteric doctrine which is designed to amaze.

- Ungodly people led by ungodly leaders will do ungodly things.

- When morality is tied to whatever is socially acceptable then society is in trouble. When whatever is socially acceptable is tied to proper morality then society will be preserved.

- The Constitution of the United States was penned by Christians and is being interpreted today by secularists. It is being perverted by humanist interpretations as they strive to make it "fit" a secular mindset.

- The devil gives no freebies.

- Every politician should strive to be able to stand before God, state his position on an issue and have God agree with him on his stance.

- It is the ingenuity and adaptability of the American people that preserves our country when our leaders do things which put us in peril. And, when we rise above their foolishness and succeed in spite of their poor leadership, they take credit for our prosperity and success. We make our poor leaders look good.

- Most people haven't been obedient enough for God to bless them enough to show them that He can do far more than they can. The disobedient always live at the level of their ability to bless themselves.

- Satan is not original in his vices from generation to generation. He just gets new material about every twenty years to try out the old lies on.

- Children used to go out to play, then, they didn't want to go out and play, now, you can't let them go out to play.

- It is a lot less trouble to "come out of the closet" than it is to clean it up.

- Just when did Christianity get to the point that it needed to "court" the world or needed to "appeal" in order to be acceptable and relevant? This is a very recent development.

- The Gospel message is denigrated when it is "marketed" like other products.

- The right to make a choice without being called discriminatory is fast vanishing. If anyone's feelings were hurt by your choice then you were discriminating.

- "Minister to" has been replaced by "satisfy."

- If man can save himself then all of God's provision in Christ was absolutely unnecessary.

- Holiness means separation; separation means removal; removal means cleansing.

- Calvinism is appealing because it is comfortable.

- The absence of hostilities is not peace.

- True peace must be between God and man, not man and man.

- Prayer is God's method of bringing over into time and history that which already exists in eternity. The resources of heaven become blessings on earth by prayer.

- Satan does not want the world to be free. He wants it to be in bondage with his people in control.

- There is a lot of difference between digging a well and digging a hole.

- You die the way you live and you are gathered to the same type of people when you die that you were like while you were alive.

- If a crowd is the goal; if it's what you want, then the world will show you how to get it. But, God's People will respond to the Bible and solid, Godly leadership. Your crowd will be smaller but it will be real.

- The world is so churchy and the church has become so worldly that one cannot tell the difference.

- Morality and spirituality are not the same thing.

- "Tolerance" is the word that the PC church has used to replace "faith."

- Life isn't about how to survive the storm but how to "dance in the rain."

- The world will give you *anything* in exchange for your soul, but God gave you *everything* for your soul.

- Satan knows how to reward his own. A person may have a "successful" existence and still lose his soul.

- B. L. O. G. often stands for: "Bullies Loving Offending Gossip."

- People let what they are going to do *after* church affect how they dress *for* church.

- When you go to worship, you are coming before God and not the world. And, when you come before God you should be different from the world.

- The pastor should set the example; not reflect the environment.

- People today think they can get saved and never break their worldly stride.

- Paul was a prisoner of Rome but he was a bond slave to Jesus Christ. Being a prisoner can end but being a bond slave to Christ lasts a lifetime.

- The righteous man knows he is a sinner; the wicked man thinks he is totally righteous.

- Christians need to stop thinking like a "church member" and start thinking like an evangelist.

- Money can buy perception but not reality. The problem is that the greater part of reality for most people is their perception of a person or an issue.

- When what you have is what you are, then you are in dire danger of losing yourself if you lose your possessions.

- "Money poor" means that all a person really has is their money. Money for the sake of money leaves one "money poor."

Quick Quotes and Pithy Sayings by William F. Harrell

- People tend to expect what the environment reflects.

- Many churches are more of a Christian organization than a Christian Organism.

- Too many preachers of today are "telling you nothing in an entertaining way."

- The right to privacy does not extend beyond one's secular life because God sees and knows everything. There is no right to privacy where God is concerned.

- Man wants to ignore the very person "by whom all things consist." So, therefore "all things are falling apart."

- The more one removes Jesus from the center of human consideration, the more things get confused and out of hand.

- Godly morality has ceased to be the measure of what we do.

- To the world, morality on an issue is not the guiding principle, but their "court granted right" is the guiding principle.

- What is "fair" is not the issue. What is morally right is the issue.

- Something which is wrong might be made legal, but that will never make it right.

- The more we consider Christ in all our endeavors the more we will operate in the realm of true rights and not in the realm of legalities.

- Man today has thrown away the Biblical world view for the secular world view.

- If God is the foundation of all truth and has truth as His character then truth is absolute because there is no variance with God. He is absolute Himself.

- For a person to hold to the view that truth is not absolute is for them to admit that they are willing to live outside of God's definition of Himself.

- You are *not* standing still. You are a resident of the earth which is rotating at 1,040 miles per hour. It is moving around the sun at about 66,486 miles per hour. The solar system (including the earth) is moving around the Milky Way galaxy at about 483,000 miles an hour. And, our Milky Way galaxy is traveling at 1.3 million miles an hour through the universe. Also the only place you can stand "up" is at the northern axis of the earth. Otherwise, you are not standing "up", you are poking out.

- Life's too easy, life's too plain, without a mountain to climb, without a battle to win ... for God.

- Show me a church which is interested in teaching and believing the Bible as well as seeking to lead its people to obedience and I will show you a church which will be under constant satanic attack.

- Rationalizing something to the point one accepts it is not the same as "God giving them peace" about the issue.

- The contemporary movement is turning Christianity into a secular religion loved by the world.

- We are being blended into the world to the point that we are no longer different.

- The church is becoming undefined because we are abandoning our distinctions—those things which identify us.

Quick Quotes and Pithy Sayings by William F. Harrell

- When "style" is the issue, then the church has become too worldly.

- We have quit wanting people to be saved as much as we want them to be fulfilled.

- The American pulpit is in trouble because it has bitten the bait.

- Any lie you tell the public, they will believe. But, tell them the truth and they will reject it.

- The world is invading the church at a rapid pace, and the church is so full of the world's people parading as Christians that they will quickly absorb anything the world tells them.

- *Joy* is given to us to take us through the times when there is no happiness.

- Our legal system now says that it's all right to be immoral; just don't break the law when doing what you do.

- Every choice one makes in life is an option, even salvation. The only thing that is not an option is physical death.

- If what you have is what you are then life for you is shallow and frustrating because you could lose who you are by losing what you have.

- People are "looking under every rock" they can to solve our problems, but the One Rock they need to consult … Jesus Christ, God's Word.

- The reason there were no liberals in Jesus' day is that He healed the dumb and the blind.

- The human body could not live if it functioned like the church.

Section Three:
Inspirational Poetry
by Elizabeth Greer Harrell
(the author's sister)

Inspirational Poetry by Elizabeth Greer Harrell

Deep Down in the Heart

"Grandmamma, Grandmamma, are you in there?"
"Yes, my child, turn the light on and come over here."

"But Grandmamma, I'm confused, why are you sitting in the dark?"
"In the dark, my child, is where I see from my heart."
"With the lights on I tend to see just what's around,
But with the lights off I focus on what's really deep down
See, 'deep down' is where the real things den
How we feel, what we think, the 'if's and might have beens.'
"And in this den that's right here,
They call it your heart,
Lies the 'real things' that matter
It's where your life gets its start."
"The days in my life are dwindling fast,
But you, my sweet child, have hardly a past."
"So, it's really important that you waste not a day
Put only good things inside
Throw the rest away."

"But how do you do that, Grandmamma," you sigh,
"You focus your eyes on the Almighty High."
"In plowing, a mule has blinders on tight
Never looks to his left … never steps to his right.
Don't listen to things that others may say,
You listen to "Him" … He'll show you the way.

And I promise you this
As the last row is plowed
As you turn and look back
You'll see a large crowd."

"You left them behind
You made your choice.
You chose in your heart
To follow God's Voice."

"Now turn off the lights
Lay your head on my chest,
We'll talk for a while
And then I must rest."

"Grandmamma, Grandmamma
I hear it so clear …
The things that you told me
Are beating right here."

"It's the heart, my sweet child
That determines that "Day"
Remember, fill it full of what's good
Then throw the rest away."

Inspirational Poetry by Elizabeth Greer Harrell

"Grandmamma, I'll always remember
    the things that you said,
I know that you're tired ...
So I'll go back to bed."
"I'm just in the next room
If something gives you a "fright."
"Oh, nothing can scare me grandmamma
Now, turn out the light."

Here's Your Daughter, Mr. Thrift

It's only been just a few short months
That God gave us a "special gift"….
And I'm sure that I "felt" the Angel's breath,
When he whispered, "Here's your daughter, Mr. Thrift."

Now the Angel wouldn't fly away …
He had much to say to me …
He wouldn't leave 'til he felt quite sure
Of the kind of father I would be.

First let me see that your arms are strong…
Can you catch her should she fall? …
And if she feels like being your "son" for the day,
Can you throw a fast curve ball?

And your hands, Mr. Thrift, are they hard and soft,
Yes, you'll need both at times don't you see?
The "hard" hand for keeping your daughter "on course" …
The "soft" for wiping her knee.

And your legs, don't forget, need to be strong as well …
They'll be used as a "pony" for a while.
and much later on you'll need "their" support …
Walking your daughter down the church aisle.

Let's look at the tops of your feet, Mr. Thrift,
For if given just half the chance ...
Little Lindsey will want to stand on them
When you're teaching her how to dance.

And your head, Mr. Thrift, can you keep it quite clear
When teaching her wrong from right?
And how will you handle the very first time
She "forgets" her curfew was midnight?

Now before I hand over our child Mr. Thrift.
I must examine the "inside" part ...
For Lindsey will make it just fine in this life ...
If her dad just has a "good" heart.

Your heart, don't you see, is what God really looks at ...
Not your legs, not your arms or your feet.
For the "things" could be taken from you in a flash ...
But in Lindsey your heart always will beat.

Don't ever forget I was sent here by God
To hand you this precious gift ...
And long, long ago He assigned her a name ...
She'll be called Miss Lindsey Joy Thrift.

You passed the test, Mr. Thrift, don't you see?
She's yours, now stretch your hands ...
For God and I both think you'll make a great dad ...
This was all part of His plan.

Inspirational Poetry by Elizabeth Greer Harrell

Make Me a Promise Granddaddy

*Make me a promise, Granddaddy,
If you get there before I do,
That you'll save me a seat up in Heaven
Cause I want to sit right next to* **you.**

*Mommy and Daddy will have seats
And Nana will have her seat too,
But no matter where they put down their seats
I want mine put right next to you.*

*They told me that Heaven's a big place,
But I'm sure that I'll never get lost,
'Cause my granddaddy will be there to guide me
No matter what the cost.*

*Yes, they say that it "cost" to get there,
But you don't pay with dollars and cents.
They tell me it's really quite easy …
They use a big word … "Repent."*

*I know that you know all those big words, Granddaddy,
But I'm really not sure that I do,
But just save me a seat up in Heaven,
Cause I want to sit right next to you!*

The Key

Today I saw a precious scene
That really touched my heart.
I want to share my thoughts with you,
Yet, I'm not sure where to start.

I saw a dear old couple,
Their actions spoke volumes to me.
After watching them only for minutes,
It was clear that their vows were the "Key."

Her dress was really quite simple,
Her hair was up in a bun.
She had to be close to ninety in years,
But I sensed she was still full of "fun."

Now, he dressed like it still was the twenties,
The sweater, the cap, just his "way."
I thought by the way he held his bride's hand
They'd surely been married that day.

They strolled to their car
And he opened "her" door.
I couldn't help but chuckle,
Not only did he "settle her in"…
He actually fastened her seat buckle!

*Oh, I could tell he loved her so much
And she was his precious gem.*

*And the "sparkle" I saw bouncing out of her eyes
Said she felt the same about him!*

*I sat there and watched
As they drove out of sight ...
My heart felt somewhat "abused."
I wish that the "vows" spoken once in my life
Had been locked with the same "key" they used.*

Your Last Day

What if today was your last day,
With no more tomorrows in sight ...
Would you kiss and hold to your loved ones?
With your brother make everything right?

What if today was your last day,
Have you done all you meant to get done?
Have you taught your child their importance,
Made your spouse feel that they're number one?

What if today was your last day,
Have you said all that needs to be said?
Have you helped your neighbor in some way,
Have you called your mother and dad?

What if today was your last day,
Have you given a gift to the poor?
Have you stopped just sitting on sidelines,
Have you tried becoming a "doer"?

Have you told someone you loved them?
Have you been there for someone in need?
Have you given a bone to a stray dog?
Have you taught someone how to read?

What if today was your last day,
God has said that it's time you must go.
Have you planted and nurtured enough Seeds,
That after you're gone some will grow?

Do you take your tomorrows for granted?
Do you think "oh, I'll have many more"?
The young man they buried this morning,
Had just "run down to the store".

Books by Free Church Press
www.freechurchpress.com

A Gentle Zephyr — A Mighty Wind: Silhouettes of Life in the Spirit, by J. Gerald Harris; Foreword by Jerry Vines. Moving messages, filled with illustrations, on the Holy Spirit.

Urgent: Igniting a Passion for Jesus, by Joe Donahue; Foreword by Ergun Caner. A powerful story how God changed one man and how God used the man to help change others. Offers a clear Gospel message.

Ancient Wine and the Bible: The Case for Abstinence, by David R. Brumbelow; Foreword by Paige Patterson. Detailed study of ancient production and kinds of wine, Scripture, and reasons for abstinence.

A Journey Through the Bible: From Genesis to Malachi, Volume I, by Jerry Vines. Introduction, outline, and synopsis of each Old Testament book by one of America's leading expositors.

A Journey Through the Bible: From Matthew to Revelation, Volume II, by Jerry Vines. Introduction, outline, and synopsis of each New Testament book.

All The Days: Daily Devotions For Busy Believers by Jerry Vines. Brief, expository devotions for every day of the year. Explores different books of the Bible from both the Old and New Testaments.

Bullseye: Perceptive Reflections on a Collapsing Culture

Green Pastures of a Barren Land: finding contentment in life's desolate seasons by Candise Farmer. After the Foreword by Kay Arthur, Candise offers Biblical encouragement to those facing difficult moments in life. In addition, Candise offers an inductive Bible study for small groups as a supplement to her book.

Straight Shooting: Pastoral Reflections for Today's Church by William "Bill" Harrell. A veteran pastor takes an honest look at the moral corruption of our culture and the church's unfortunate failure to stop it.

Born Guilty? A Southern Baptist View of Original Sin by Adam Harwood. Dr. Harwood makes the clear biblical distinction between "imputed sinful guilt" and "inherited sinful nature" and shows why it's significant for believers today. The first booklet in an exclusive teaching series by Free Church Press.

What is Calvinism? everything you need to know about Calvinism... and then some by Peter Lumpkins. The author answers the question concerning what Calvinism is, then shows Calvinism's inadequacy as a theological system to be imposed upon Scripture. *What is Calvinism?* is a part of an exclusive teaching series by Free Church Press specifically written for those without a theological background.

Preach The Word! A Collection of Essays on Biblical Preaching in Honor of Jerry Vines, edited by David L. Allen and Peter Lumpkins. Contributors include a "Who's Who" among Southern Baptists–Paige Patterson, O. S. Hawkins, Mac Brunson, Steve Smith, Malcolm Yarnell, Stephen Rummage, Steve Lemke, Johnny Hunt, Emir and Ergun Caner among many others. This essay collection may define Biblical preaching from a Southern Baptist perspective for years to come.

www.ingramcontent.com/pod-product-compliance
Lightning Source LLC
LaVergne TN
LVHW051837080426
835512LV00018B/2936